Uncommon Virtue

Raoul Plus, S.J.

Uncommon Virtue
Everyday Methods for Attaining Spiritual Excellence

Translated from the French
by
Sister Mary Edgar Meyer, O.S.F.

SOPHIA INSTITUTE PRESS
Manchester, New Hampshire

Copyright © 2021 by Raoul Plus, S.J.

Previously published in 1950 by The Newman Press, Westminster, Maryland

Printed in the United States of America. All rights reserved.

Cover design: Theresa Blume with Sophia Institute Press

Cover art: Praying hands with rosary (1278500008)
(c) vectorgreen / shutterstock.com

No part of this book may be reproduced, stored in a retrieval system, or transmitted in any form, or by any means, electronic, mechanical, photocopying, or otherwise, without the prior written permission of the publisher, except by a reviewer, who may quote brief passages in a review.

Sophia Institute Press
Box 5284, Manchester, NH 03108
1-800-888-9344

www.SophiaInstitute.com

Sophia Institute Press® is a registered trademark of Sophia Institute.

Nihil Obstat:

EDWARD A. CERNY, S.S., D.D.

Censor Librorum

Imprimatur:

FRANCIS P. KEOUGH, D.D.

Archbishop of Baltimore

March 13, 1950

paperback ISBN 978-1-64413-646-1

ebook ISBN 978-1-64413-647-8

Library of Congress Control Number: 2022930319

First printing

Contents

	Introduction 1
I.	Knowing How to be Grateful 3
	Gratitude is rare .4
	Why? 4
	Why the act of thanksgiving? 8
	Examples of grateful souls 10
	Gratitude in time of trial 11
	The most favorable moment for thanksgiving . . . 12
II.	Love of Recollection 15
	Suggested texts 18
	Usefulness of silence 23
	What degree of recollection can we attain? 26
	Opportune information 29
	What is meant by praying always? 32
	It is true 35
III.	Good Use of Time 37
	The obsession of saving time 37
	Proper decorum 39
	Necessary relaxation 45
	Conclusion 52
IV.	The Spirit of Discretion 53
	As a simply human quality 54
	In the moral domain 56
	Danger of indiscreet fervor 64
	But the excess of the saints? 66

V.	Facing Life	71
	Courage	71
	To proceed slowly	74
	Maintain serenity in everything	76
	Fidelity to the duties of our state of life	79
	Heaven helps those who help themselves	82
	To know how to endure	89
	In company with the Cyrenean	94
VI.	Magnanimity in Suffering	101
	Grappling with ill-health	101
	Some examples	106
	Two names among many	111
	Henri d'Hellencourt	111
	André Bach	118
VII.	Love of Reparation	129
	The problem	130
	"I fill up"	134
	Pius XI and Margaret Mary	137
	The practice of reparation	144
VIII.	Pity for the Sick and Afflicted	149
	An Invalid, Apostle of Invalids	149
	In the service of those who suffer	158
	Seekers of love	159
	The most forsaken	164
	About the Author	169

Introduction

All virtues are rare. Some are especially rare, perhaps because they possess a more delicate grain. Or perhaps there may be lacking first of all a soil of special quality, a more particularly rich ensemble of human and supernatural gifts, which is needed so that they may bloom.

We should like to study briefly a few examples of these virtues. We have chosen gratitude, the spirit of recollection, the art of using time, discretion, courage in facing life, magnanimity in suffering, love of reparation, pity for those who suffer, and the apostolic spirit even to the gift of oneself.

These essays are not learned studies, designed for the use of psychologists or professional moralists. They are very simple essays, varied in length, for the use of souls of good will who, in acquiring one or the other of these virtues, have met with practical difficulties which they did not expect.

Sometimes is it less a question of a supernatural virtue, strictly speaking, than of a quality of a human order, a

Uncommon Virtue

quality, moreover, worth developing because it will contribute much to growth in the spiritual life.

Here and there, when the subject seemed to lend itself more readily, we have given illustrations. At certain times, they are more persuasive than the most beautiful theories.

I

Knowing How to be Grateful

A soul who was blessed by God in an extraordinary manner, Marie-Antoinette de Geuser,[1] once wrote these lines: "By my correspondence to grace at every moment, I should like to increase in love in the full measure of the gift which the Lord grants me, in order to be for Him a living act of thanksgiving. Our heavenly Father has sketched our life. It seems to me that I see my every moment prepared in advance with an infinite love. I am like the little child who tries with all his heart to trace the written pages prepared by his mother." At the same time that she applies herself with a perfect fidelity, she exults with an inexpressible

---

[1] In addition to her *Vie* (Toulouse: Apostolat de la Prière) and the *Lettres de Marie de la Trinité* (Carmel d'Avignon), we may read with profit the fine doctoral dissertation by M.-Th. Guignet (Paris: Desclée de Brouwer).

gratitude. More recently, we have read in the *Testament Spirituel* of the lamented Msgr. Chaptal: "The day when I shall leave this earth, I wish that my last thought be to say once more to the good God, *Thank you.*" It is dated May 2, 1940, when the prelate was almost eighty years old.

Gratitude is rare

Why is it that such delicate sentiments are not found in every soul? Alas! We recall the ten lepers who were cured by the good Master but left for home so soon after the miracle. Only one of them sees that such conduct is unbecoming and returns to give thanks to our Lord. "And the other nine?" Jesus cannot refrain from asking. The other nine? They disappeared without leaving any trace!

Why?

To explain the little gratitude that we have toward God, there are reasons that depend on the actions of divine Providence and those which depend on our innate indifference.

God showers blessings upon us every moment, but He does it without revealing Himself. We do not see Him act. He is there, behind the screen of second causes. But because He who is the first cause of everything is hidden, we attend only to the gifts He grants. The figure of the

Knowing How to be Grateful

donor, His hands, His heart, escape us. God preserves us in existence at every moment. For this, as much power is needed, according to our way of speaking, as was required at the time of our origin to create us out of nothing. Who gives any thought to this fact? If from this example taken in the natural order, we then pass to the supernatural order, who thinks at the time of a child's baptism of an unheard-of marvel? The Blessed Trinity comes to take its abode, without a sound but nevertheless really, in this weak, whimpering creature? A priest consecrates, and the little bell rings for the elevation. I ask you, who even among the fervent realizes fully the sublime beauty of what has taken place? Are we not all more or less like the patriarch Jacob? He stretches himself out on the ground in the evening, and God sends him the great vision of the ladder. In the morning he awakens, and not seeing anything extraordinary around him, the landscape having remained unchanged from the evening before, he cries out, "Indeed the Lord is in this place, and I knew it not." (Gen. 28:16). God is everywhere around us and works for us incessantly, but we do not notice Him.

Not only is God's dispensation of His benefits invisible, but for our benefit, it goes on uninterruptedly. On our part, this should be the chief reason for being grateful. Psychologically, in fact, one scarcely appreciates what one receives in the usual way. Light comes to us every morning; our heart drives the blood in our veins every fraction of a second; our lungs take in at every respiration the oxygen which continually bathes us. Who thinks of thanking God? Ah! If there is a cessation, if the gift for one reason or other is broken off, we learn by its loss that it was a gift.

Furthermore, our lack of courtesy is such that instead of thanking God for the times when He granted us His munificence, most frequently, we can only complain when He has temporarily withdrawn this munificence.

Weighed down as we are with material things, even we, the faithful, lack a spirit of faith. Preoccupied with worldly affairs, immersed in the things of sense, we have great difficulty in rising to things spiritual. Not only are we wanting in interior sensibility, but we are wanting in love. Our hearts are small; we gain possession of something we have coveted. Perfect! We forget all the rest.

Here we touch on the principal obstacle: the absence of the filial spirit, the spirit that must mark the children of God. We often say to the Lord that He is *Our Father*; but that is a mere formula. A well-trained child receives nothing from his parents without saying immediately: "Thank

Knowing How to be Grateful

you, Papa! Thank you, Mama!" In our childhood days, if it happened that we were carried away by the beauty or value of a gift and forgot its giver, a voice asked: "What do you say?" If we were content to stammer out only the word "Thanks," the voice again asked: "Thanks to whom?" It was very necessary then, willingly or unwillingly—let us hope that it was always willingly—to proclaim the title of the benefactor. It is not without difficulty that we have learned how to be grateful to people.

Do children in every Christian home learn how to say "Thank you" to God? Fr. Faber rightly notes how we importune God when we want to obtain a favor! After having received it, in what proportion do we express our gratitude?[2] The failure to express thanks is not, like sin, an offense against God by those who are His enemies. It is an offense committed by those who call themselves His friends but whose love is too imperfect to rise to disinterestedness. In Heaven, the principal prayer of the elect is the prayer of thanksgiving together with that of adoration. We should live as much as possible as if we were already in Heaven, seeking the glory of God rather than our own

---

[2] See F. W. Faber, *Notes on Doctrinal and Spiritual Subjects* (London, 1866), ii, 42. See also *All for Jesus*, ch. vii.

little personal advantages and bursting into gratitude for His benefits. The act of thanksgiving is one of the most perfect forms of the cult of love.

Why the act of thanksgiving?

A modern author has made this statement: "If anyone were able to recall, were it only for a second, all the details of any scene of his childhood, he would fall dead from sadness." Such pessimism toward the past! Would it not be much more correct to say, "He would fall into an ecstasy of gratitude?"

What benefits have not been showered upon us, and at every moment, at every period of our life![3] He has given us general benefits, that is, those which have been granted us in common with our fellow men. Some are natural benefits: the air which we breathe, the light by which we see, the nourishment which sustains our life. Someone has written the *History of a Mouthful of Bread* in order to explain to children the complexity of human labor. Why did he not write it to show God's laborious concern to lavish

---

[3] The booklet *Comment bien prier*, in the chapters on *La prière de remerciement*, goes into more detail than is possible here. We refer the reader to it.

upon us maternal care? What are we to say of supernatural benefits, of that which constitutes divine life within us, the gift of sanctifying grace to Adam at the beginning of the world? And after Adam lost all by Original Sin, the more beautiful restoration of it — *melius reformasti* — of the divine in the human, with all that it includes, the coming of the Word of God on earth, the Virgin Mary, and the Church, with its teaching authority which protects the faith and its sacraments to nourish it?

"If during our whole life," St. Gregory of Nyssa used to say, "we conversed with God without the least distraction, and if we did nothing but express our gratitude to Him, we would be far from counterbalancing our thanks with His benefits for the shortest instant of time." Nothing is more true. Only benefits are accorded to all of us. How can one count the particular favors distributed by God to each one: the gift of life,[4] the blessing of a Christian country, the good examples given, the temptations warded off, the sacraments received, the sermons heard, the interior inspirations, the holy aspirations, the possibilities and fruitfulness of the apostolate?

[4] "I thank God for my existence," said Katherine Mansfield, the novelist.

Uncommon Virtue

Examples of grateful souls

However little we may be in the habit of meditating on the goodness of God, we know that Fr. Martinez, a Peruvian Jesuit, had trained himself to say *Deo gratias* four hundred times a day and encouraged others to do the same; that St. Paul never separated from his prayer that of thanksgiving, as if for him there could be no real prayer if the act of thanksgiving was not connected with it; that St. Paul of the Cross, touching with his cane the flowers along the road, entreated them at least to excite in him gratitude to God; that St. Gertrude devoted the sixth of her *Exercises* to giving thanks; that St. Ignatius of Loyola prescribed, in the examination of conscience, which he recommends to be made twice a day, that we should train ourselves to be grateful by the examination of the mercies of God on our behalf, and we know that he himself not only thanked God for graces received but even thanked for those graces which God would not have failed to bestow on numerous persons if they had deigned to correspond to grace. Dominating all these is the Virgin Mary as she sings her *Magnificat.*

It can be said without deceiving ourselves that the lives of most of the saints are a perpetual *Deo gratias.* On the contrary, when the supernatural begins to ebb, sighs and complaints begin.

Gratitude in time of trial

When a trial is sent to us, it is more difficult than at other times to know how to be thankful to God. We need to acquire sufficient supernatural strength in order to believe that God remains a Father when He makes us feel the weight of the Cross. Behind the suffering that occupies the foreground, we must learn to discover the heart of the One who, by this trial, wishes either to make us grow more spiritually, to permit us to expiate our sins, or to identify us more with His divine Son and to make us participate more fully in the Redemption.

An admirable example is found in the grandmother of Msgr. de Ségur, Countess Rostopchine, who embraced Catholicism at the age of forty. Having learned at ninety about the blindness that had come upon the prelate, she wrote to him: "Happy Gaston, for having entered into the life of the blessed announced by the Savior! The God of our souls treats you as one of His elect: He takes away your sight; He illumines your soul."

Such ought to be always the attitude of souls who have faith. Let us listen here again to the saints. St. Margaret

Uncommon Virtue

Mary blessed God for the sufferings He sent her: "On my behalf, thank our sovereign Master for honoring me so lovingly and liberally with His precious Cross!... What shall I render to the Lord for the great benefits that He bestows on me?" St. Teresa rejoices when God prevents the realization of one or the other of her plans for a foundation; St. Francis of Assisi encourages his companion to thank God if it happens to both of them to be refused everywhere!

The most favorable moment for thanksgiving

It is a good practice to offer each day to God in thanksgiving with an intention that we have previously determined upon. On Sunday, we should thank God for favors received personally or granted by God throughout in the world; on Monday, for certain other favors; and so on.

The most favorable moment to show our gratitude to God is during that which Christian usage has justly called the act of thanksgiving, that is, the time which follows the reception of Holy Communion.

"Eucharist" signifies "thanksgiving." Having infinite value, the Mass constitutes for the sovereign Majesty at one and the same time the best act of adoration, of reparation, and of supplication, and it is the most perfect demonstration of thanksgiving. Our Savior, the divine elder brother, offers to His Father, in His name and in our name, at the time of the renewal of His Sacrifice, the homage of His gratitude and of ours for the incomparable gift of supernatural life and of the Redemption.[5]

Fr. Lancicius, a sixteenth-century Polish Jesuit, recalled a legend of the ancient Jews: When God had finished His creation, He asked the angels what they thought of the work of His hands. One of them replied that the world was so vast and so perfect that there was nothing wanting, except a voice to offer to the Most High, in an unceasing hymn of praise, the expression of a gratitude due to Him. Were these angels ignorant of how Christ in the Mass one day was to surpass their desires?

To St. Bridget, our Savior explained: "My Body is immolated every day on the altar in order that men may love Me more and more each day and may recall more often My benefits to them."

May it please God that our thanksgivings after Holy Communion be especially devoted to express our

---

[5] Note that in the liturgy of more than one Mass is found the act of thanksgiving, for example, Pentecost Tuesday (introit); Sunday in the octave of the Ascension (postcommunion); feast of St. Louis of Gonzaga (postcommunion), etc.

gratitude. We need not deny ourselves the prayer of petition. But much more we should exert ourselves to give thanks. We should unite our gratitude to that which our Lord Himself offers to the Most High when He has just renewed out of love for us and for the glorification of His Father the sacrifice of His Calvary. That will render us most pleasing to God, and by subterfuge, as it were, it will most effectually draw upon us favors from Heaven.[6] Let us be more forgetful of ourselves than we have been in the past. Our great preoccupation must be the glory of God, and the best object of our gratitude must be the very grandeur of that infinite God. The best thanksgiving is that which is not concerned with the benefits which we have received but with the glory that God shows forth for Himself. It is for us to make more and more our own the words of the *Gloria* of the Mass which St. Paul of the Cross had for his favorite invocation: "We give Thee thanks, O Lord, for Thy greater glory!"

[6] St. Bernard very fittingly observes: "Express to God your thanks and you will receive from Him more and more abundant graces." This does not mean that we should learn to thank God only or chiefly in view of obtaining new favors from Him. The great value of the act of thanksgiving consists in its being a disinterested prayer.

II

Love of Recollection

When Beethoven's brother had *Landbesitzer*, "landed proprietor," printed on his visiting cards, the famous musician had *Hirnbesitzer*, "brain proprietor," printed on his.

Assuredly, not everyone can boast of possessing a mind like that of the great Beethoven. But everyone should desire to make the best use of the mind that he has. Alas! How limited is the number of those who deign to think! The distracting noise of countless occupations and the craze for uncurbed activity have killed the taste for quiet and reflection, the silence and freedom of spirit necessary for recollection. We are preoccupied with external things; we never retire within ourselves.

When Léon Bérard was Undersecretary of State for Fine Arts, he wrote a preface to Ajalbert's *Dix années à Malmaison*. Among other suggestions with regard to reform in the French government, he proposed a resolution "that ministers should be given twenty-four hours a week to inform themselves of what is done in all the offices under their authority, an hour every morning to see their principal officials, an hour every evening not to see anyone and to reflect."

Let us omit the twenty-four hours destined to inspect the various offices under their administration and the hour each morning for meeting the staff. Let us keep only the request for a single hour each evening for reflection. This should be decreed by law, that is to say, administratively, by public authority, and not left to good luck or to the good will of the officer in charge, who is a prey to all the risks of a life overrun by business, useful or useless receptions, speeches to be prepared, and so on.

Ministers are not the only people who are overburdened with work. What profession gives to those who exercise it the possibility of looking back? No one grants himself the alms of a little pause. With the time that flies, we hasten along. Never a minute to breathe.

In the minister's daily administrative schedule, one would be able to anticipate, according to law, an hour of silence each evening: If it is a question of private persons, how can one imagine statutes compelling them? Everyone is left to his own initiative. How many grant themselves the indispensable?

Reflect? I have too many other things to do!

Bérard asked for one hour. Suppose we would say half of that. Would you consent if it were a question of only a half hour? Ah, you think, *do you really expect to see me have a tête-à-tête with myself for a half hour? Do not think of it!* Very well; let us make it a quarter of an hour. Who could not, at the suspension of all other business, give himself a quarter of an hour of serious meditation every day? Fifteen minutes out of one thousand four hundred and forty minutes; do not say that you could not! *It is not that I could not, but that I do not want to; it means nothing to me!*

"Could" is a great word! I *could*! Many men *could*! Some at least could, if they would only listen to our plea to take this blessed and fruitful bit of rest. But this they do not want to do.

Far from being time gained for the exercise of their work, whatever it may be, this refusal to spare time for needed reflection is an immense detriment.

Here is a significant confession of Dr. Paul Tournier in his *Médecine de la personne:*[7] "The doctor who no longer

[7] (Neuchâtel: Delachaux et Niestlé), p. 60.

finds in the course of the day an opportunity to retire within himself, to exercise his own interior life, to prepare his consultations in prayer and in meditating on his patients under the inspiration of God, cannot bring them the spiritual atmosphere necessary for their complete confidence. Carried away by his practical devotion, he leads a fatiguing and unsatisfied life in which are rarely found the peaceful and vast opportunities for giving his patient what the latter expects most from him."

Wilbois, who made a special study of the problems of training youth, puts a half hour of meditation in the daily schedule of every student in quest of personal activity. He explains how this "reflection, without words, upon things and oneself," can and must be practiced, and he concludes: "A businessman who would meditate on his affairs thirty minutes every evening would see his thoughts fall as golden rain. In every family, in every school, in every factory, it should be made a strict obligation."[8]

Suggested texts

Authorities are not wanting who encourage setting aside for oneself sufficient time for reflection.

[8] *La Nouvelle Education Française* (Payot), pp. 125-128.

Love of Recollection

A young noncommissioned officer, who amuses himself and has not found his point of equilibrium, is asked by a commander who is also his friend: "Have you ever, in all your life, remained alone more than an hour or two? If you take pleasure in communing with yourself, you are a strong man." As the officer does not refuse to attempt what is depicted as so fruitful for him, his mentor continues: "You must find how important an experience it is."

Even Maeterlinck, the author of *The Blue Bird* and *The Life of the Bee*, extols interior silence. "We speak," he writes, "only during the time when we do not live.... We use a great part of our life seeking the places where silence does not reign. As soon as two or three persons meet, they think only of banishing the invisible enemy, for how many friendships have no other foundation than the hatred of silence!"[9] He appeals to the benefits which we have been able to reap from some very rare opportunities for recollection: "Recall the day when you met without fear your first silence. That was ... on the return from a trip, on the threshold of a departure, in the course of a great joy, beside a corpse, or on the brink of a misfortune.... Tell me whether the caresses of the enemy were

---

[9] Maurice Maeterlinck, *The Treasure of the Humble*, ch. 1.

not then divine caresses?" What do we know about a man who lives always occupied with external things? To this, Maeterlinck answers: "We cannot form an exact idea of one who has never kept silence. One would say that his soul has not had any sight." A little later he adds: "Souls weigh themselves in silence."

We have a better authority in Paul Claudel.[10] In spite of the multiple duties of an ambassador's life, he knew how to find time for opportune recollection. Skilled in handling the texts of Scripture, he never misses the opportunity to invite his readers to the refreshing and fruitful work of meditation. Listen to him as he glosses the words of Ecclesiasticus, *non impedias musicam* (32:5): "do not hinder, by giving too much attention to interior tumults, the divine music from the depths of your soul"; or the text of Isaiah, in the liturgy of the Saturday after Ash Wednesday, *loqui quod non prodest* (58:9): "Avoid speaking of that which is useless."

"It is a question of this incessant welling up in us of images, words, thoughts, memories, ideas, and trifles. Our mind is a winnowing basket which sifts and resifts all that."

---

[10] See Paul Claudel, *La Présence de Dieu*, in *La Vie spirituelle*, October 1, 1932, text republished in his book, *Présence et Prophétie*.

Love of Recollection

Calling to his aid Exodus, Proverbs, and the book of Kings, he observes: "Exodus tells us that the river brought forth an abundance of frogs. The river is our everyday life. The frogs are the vain words posted on the riparian marsh which do not cease to make their deafening note heard." Again, if it were only a question of frogs, it would be one thing; but elsewhere, it is a question of an "abundance of mice," and these little animals devour the grain of the sower: "It is necessary that the repose of the Sabbath reigns from one end to the other of the interior mansions of our soul, a sacred rest, a delicate and exquisite suspension."

Who will deliver us from useless words, from those idle words which our Lord condemned, from all those empty conversations in which so much precious time is consumed, from the trash on the radio, from the claptrap of charlatans, from news having either no foundation or a false one?

Give us time to think!

No! There is always someone to drive us again into the uproar. At the age of eight, Félicité de La Mennais often ran away from home in order to contemplate the sea. As soon as the maid discovered his flight, she hastened to him: "Come, come Master Féli. You have looked enough. The storm is over. Besides, you see everybody is going away!"

Uncommon Virtue

Everybody! That is the real reason; everybody chatters. Then I, too, ought to excuse myself from returning to the common resort of gossips. It would be so useful, however, to look behind the words and to seek to discover what they conceal. While still young, we quickly, too quickly, learned the names of things. "What is that, Papa?" Then father gave us a word, and we were contented with it. We no longer sought to contemplate the real thing; the word sufficed. We enriched our vocabulary but lessened our capacity for observation and reflection.

Now and then, it is true, words can help us arrive at the knowledge of things: "Look at this expression! What does it mean?" Happy are those who have recourse to the dictionary or make inquiries. The majority dispense themselves from all investigation and refuse to enrich their knowledge. We all must accuse ourselves of this indolence.

It is not that speaking is unpleasant and unprofitable. We must not act in a sullen manner. Contact with those among our fellow men who are like ourselves is pleasant; we are created to live in society. It is enriching. *Scio abundare, scio esurire.* But there is a time to talk, and a time to be silent. "Whenever I have been in society, I loved it as if I could not stand seclusion," Montesquieu used to say. But he adds: "Whenever I was at home, I no longer thought about society."

Love of Recollection

Usefulness of silence

Many never go home; that is, they never enter within themselves. And yet, how great is the value of silence, that replenishing silence in which thought seeks contact with the real and the invisible? Without it, the interior life is impossible.

We consider here two words, "silence" and "interior life," in the broadest sense: silence not only of words but of the imagination and of sensibility, silence with others when charity, politeness, and the duty of our state do not command otherwise, and, even more, silence within ourselves; interior life, that is to say, not an existence in which everything is decided by the exterior or by caprice but an existence in which one is the master of himself and reserves for himself some time to think.

Baudelaire used to say, "I grew up through leisure." He was not speaking of that indolence which can only waste time; he was speaking of the time devoted to interior reflection. We, too, can grow up through silence, through the habit of keeping silence, of asking ourselves useful questions interiorly about persons, events, or things, of giving ourselves interiorly the solutions discovered, of seeking to put into practice and to our advantage the remedies disclosed to us.

Uncommon Virtue

"The less one has of the interior life, the more things seem easy," once wrote the Danish philosopher Kierkegaard. That is: the less one reflects, the more one is ignorant of the complexity of problems. So many people speak who evidently do not know the first word about what they are saying. Be silent! Study, learn to think: you will get a clear idea that all is not simple, that it is necessary to turn your tongue around in your mouth seven times before you speak, and that after the seventh time, the best thing still to do is to take up the problem again in order to examine it more thoroughly. The more we possess the interior life, the more the difficulty of the solutions appears. Hence the anguished and primordial question: "Do I have any responsibility for what happens? I express my appreciation, I criticize, but am I involved in this case? Others, of course, but I? Am I the one for whom the world is waiting and of whom it has need?"

To keep silence is to renounce remaining a mere nonentity; it is to obligate ourselves not to remain stagnant and to prepare for building something solid. "Do you wish to build?" our Lord asks. Go into seclusion and make some serious estimates, calculate your expenses, draw up the balance-sheet of possible gains. When you begin the work, the undertaking will not baffle you, and you will know how to build.

Love of Recollection

Silence filled with prudent reflections is fruitful for the interior life understood in its broadest sense. This fruitfulness reaches its maximum potential if one takes the expression "interior life" in its richest and most precise meaning: namely, union with God.

Spiritual writers agree in their praise of meditation, mental prayer, and silent prayer. If they are discreet, pastors do not simply require their parishioners to follow instructions. They also require attentive reflection on the words heard, for this is the only means of making the word of God penetrate our souls. "After my sermon," St. Bernardine of Siena was wont to say, "imitate the ox: ruminate, ruminate, ruminate!" Many souls would become great if they had resolved not to remain always within their own periphery! Many pious souls would be stronger, more tender, and more animated if they had better sought God in the active silence of an attentive soul. St. Vincent de Paul did not hesitate to say, "Give me a man of prayer, and he will be capable of doing anything." Enlarging the horizon, he adds—and his proposal is valuable for every individual or group that aspires to do anything—"The Congregation of the Mission will last as long as the exercise of prayer is faithfully practiced in it."

If one wishes particularly to make contact with the invisible Host, *dulcis hospes animae*, one must go and visit Him there where He is found. Many souls, even very supernatural souls, pass near the great secret and are subject to the reproaches which Charles du Bos addressed to himself: "At forty," he wrote, "I am still centering myself on the center," and he regrets having "treated the points of the periphery too much as centers," that is, leaving the devotion which should be first in preference to those which are secondary or adventitious. He had the feeling "that the main altar of his spiritual life remained vacant, and that he had given too much attention to the side chapels." Rightly he concludes: "Henceforth only the high altar will be important for me."

But here, a grave problem presents itself.

What degree of recollection can we attain?

For fervent souls, and especially for converts who have just discovered the reality of the invisible world, it is necessary to keep in contact with God. They perceived in their prayers that the Lord is the unique good, hence they desire that the majesty of this good be perpetually present to them, either under the form of a sweetness dwelling in the depth of their being and accompanying them in the midst of the most worldly occupations, or under the form of a consciousness in a way more or less clear or obscure but always present.

Love of Recollection

Of the first case, we may have an example in Jacques Rivière, who, although still very young, was the director of the *Nouvelle Revue Française* in 1914, and who returned to the faith, or at any rate, to its practice and to a rare degree, during his captivity at Königsbrück.[11] His wife, Isabel, who knew him and the nature of his spiritual needs after his return to God, observed: "With his nature, which could never pause, the most subtly difficult problem which a soul like his finds is not at all that of believing, but of being able, in the moments when grace deserts you, to continue to believe while continuing to feel being alive." — "In the moments when grace deserts you" — it is not a question of grace "completely absent," since grace never deserts a heart which seeks it, but of grace not felt.

Charles du Bos, from whom we have already cited an interesting confidence, speaks in clear terms on the second case in his *Journal*, dated December 14, 1927. In the midst of his ordinary occupations, he reproached himself for "having been away from" his faith. "How am I to explain that? It is not that I have had doubts or a crisis of an

---

[11] Alain Fournier's sister, the wife of Jacques Rivière, published the memorandum books of her husband's captivity under the title *A la Trace de Dieu*, after his premature death. It is very interesting reading.

intellectual or even spiritual order. It is simply that *I have, I dare say, forgotten that I believed.*" It is he who emphasizes these words. He continues: "It was produced in me on a generalized scale.... The reason for reproaching myself was that in the course of my work, I no longer thought of God; I no longer thought of anything but my work." It seems to him that in what concerns him, "faith depends entirely on a continuous consciousness of the invisible world."

Because of the state of his health, which imposed on him a necessary confinement and thus gave him a greater opportunity for interior silence, or because of a faith which he needed to acquire and which he nourished with the strong substance of spiritual reading, Charles du Bos was better equipped than many others. He confesses: "When I visualize the invisible, I believe, and when I do not visualize it, I am the more culpable; for, on all planes, I live and can live in the invisible, which is, properly speaking, my element." Alas! In spite of this ability, which is a rare gift, he reproaches himself for having too often forgotten himself. "When I cease to visualize the invisible, not only am I no longer conscious of believing, but I forget that I believe." He aspires to a continual *presence of the invisible.* It is he, again, who emphasizes these words.

Love of Recollection

The firmness of his faith is not in question. "My faith is the coronation of all that I think about everything, of all that I feel about everything, of all that I wish about everything. But ... on the plane of habit, my faith is a child. I allude here to the mysterious contradiction between assent and practice. Assent, in so far as it is assent, can be complete. Practice is like the rock of Sisyphus, which had to be rolled back again every day." He desires that in his work, "specifically religious activity may be called upon as much as possible."

Opportune information

To recall these two cases leads us to give some useful and precise information.

To believe is not to have at every moment present in one's mind the reasons for belief. We know that faith rests on solid motives; that suffices. Nor does to believe mean to have a savory, sensible, felt consciousness of the very object of belief. We can remain dry and cold and still retain a faith that is serious, efficacious, and rich in potentialities. Moreover, we can suffer the blow of doubts more or less severe and still preserve our faith intact. Just as trees shaken by the wind drive their roots more deeply into the soil, so a faith shaken by temptations often becomes more firmly rooted in the soul. To believe is to want to believe, just as to love is to want to love and not merely to feel that one loves.

This explains Rivière's case, at least in part.

As to the desires expressed by du Bos, let us recall some principles.

Writers distinguish between two kinds of contemplation: infused contemplation and acquired contemplation. In the first, the soul enjoys the benefit of a particular and entirely gratuitous grace and finds God easily, without thinking of it. Even when she does not dream of thinking about Him, God surrounds her, occupies her, and manifests Himself to her more or less clearly and lastingly, for there are different degrees of infused contemplation. Of itself, human effort is powerless to obtain a similar favor; it belongs to the world of the preternatural. To one person, God gives such a grace; to another, perhaps as deserving, the Lord does not give it, for reasons known only to Him. The question of knowing whether, after having lived a long time in complete fidelity, one is introduced officially into "the storerooms of the King," at the time chosen by the Most High, is debated among spiritual writers. All agree in affirming that there is no connection "by right" between this fidelity, even though it is complete and prolonged,

Love of Recollection

and obtaining these graces of the mystic order. They do not agree on the question of whether God does in fact grant them always to those who do not refuse anything to grace for a considerable time and do not cease to aspire to the most intimate union by all the means in their power. Because of many seemingly exceptional cases, certain spiritual masters do not dare to say that in that case, God will always grant the graces of infused contemplation. Others are more categorical and do not hesitate in favor of the affirmative. *Adhuc sub judice lis est.*[12]

Let us leave the problem of infused contemplation. Left to the resources of single ordinary graces and without the intervention of gratuitous favors, *gratis datae*, to what can a soul, every soul, attain?

Let us explain it clearly. Apart from the case of infused contemplation, it is impossible to acquire a continual remembrance of God. We need our whole mind in order to attend to the occupation of the moment, especially if it demands any intellectual effort. How, then, can we attend to two operations at the same time: the supposed absorbing action of the moment, and another action, delicate in itself, which consists in fixing the attention on God? When

---

[12] "The case is still before the court."

we were in college, our old Father Rector used to tell us: "Do your best; that will always be bad enough!" That was a striking way of telling us to direct all our attention to the action of the moment. Even then, we do not always obtain marvelous results.

We wish it were possible to do at the same time two things which are very difficult: to attend to the action of the moment and to have God present to us! Whoever has applied himself to prayer for a little while has discovered that even when every other matter ceased and every other activity was deliberately excluded, he did not always get happy results. *A fortiori*, it would be presumptuous to expect an intense application to the invisible in the midst of multiple duties that keep us in touch with the sensible world and sometimes immerse us in it. To do a thing well is a rare success; to succeed well in two things at the same time is an impossibility.

What is meant by praying always?

As we have tried to explain elsewhere, when our Lord bade us "to pray always,"[13] He did not mean to ask us to

[13] See under this title a little booklet published by the Apostolat de la Prière, 9, rue Monplaisir, Toulouse.

Love of Recollection

be constantly in *the act* of prayer but only to live in *the state* of prayer. Let us note the difference: to be constantly in the act of prayer would be to fill our life's course with religious exercises alone! After prayer, Mass; after Mass, the Rosary; after the Rosary, spiritual reading; and so on. Even in the most contemplative lives, this is never done. There is always a place for certain activities that are more or less secular: meals, recreations, sleep, and the like. Living in a state of prayer does not aim at an impossible existence. The part of our lives devoted to religious exercises will mean that in all things, although it might be a question of a secular action, we will have no other purpose than to give glory to God. What we will seek along with these secular activities, which often constitute the most obvious duties of our state of life, will be less to have our *attention* always fixed on God than always to have an *intention* directed as much as possible toward God.

Attention is a necessary condition for devoting ourselves well to prayer. Intention is the best means to make everything a prayer. When it is a matter of pious exercise, what is asked of me is to try to seize my forces so as to direct them to God. It is established that as a general rule, the intellect must be gained in order that the heart may be inflamed and the will may be resolved. When it is no longer a question of a religious exercise but of an activity of a secular kind, what is asked of me is not so much to think of God as to work for God. To work for God is the intention of desiring His glory in all things. But if thinking of God would hinder me from accomplishing perfectly an action by absorbing my mind too much, I ought to force myself to reject the thought of God. Above all, I must do what I am doing and do it well. This will be with the maximum of love but not necessarily with a love that is explicitly expressed or "realized" to the maximum degree.

Let me say with St. Ignatius of Loyola, "All for the greater glory of God!" Or with Marie-Antoinette de Ceuser, "I shall put in the least of my actions the same love as for going to martyrdom." Then, in the most unconstrained way, and in a way that is most "free from everything, save Jesus Christ," let me do as well as possible the work demanded by the duty of my vocation in life. If this activity, thoroughly and vigorously performed, permits me to turn to God from time to time, so much the better! But supposing it does not leave me the opportunity to do so? There is no reason for blaming oneself for that; it is a result of the force of circumstances, or rather, of the weakness of the memory. A humorous definition of this faculty has been given. "Memory is the faculty of forgetting." I forgot! A lucky mishap! You come under the common rule.

It is true

It is true that if by a wise self-discipline, by a habitual training in interior silence when a necessary or useful activity does not claim us, by the conscientious fidelity to the moments of loving attention to God, which are the exercises of piety, especially prayer, we aspired more to be less occupied with external things—*effusus ad exteriora*, as the *Imitation of Jesus Christ* says—we would acquire much greater facility than we think in turning to God often in the course of our stated duties.

Saintly and prudent prelates, such as Msgr. Dupanloup and Msgr. d'Hulst, reproached themselves for sacrificing too much for the many tasks that consumed their lives. "I do too many things," the first reproached himself at every retreat, and the second: "The activities of life carry me away!" If there is a form of natural activity that is a gift from God—woe to the indolent, the fallen asleep, the lazy!—there is another form of activity that is the great stumbling-block in the search for recollection. We like to reach a state of contemplation before setting out for it; we do not allow ourselves time "to purify the intention," we deliver ourselves as prey to an activity that is much more the satisfaction of caprice than a work exclusively performed for God. With great common sense, serious spiritual writers are severe toward this unhappy tendency. Even when one knows perfectly how to conduct himself, it remains a fact that he cannot change his nature, and it is rash to expect from himself more than he is psychologically able to do.

Without doubt, this is what the Abbé Altermann explained to Charles du Bos in order to calm his anxiety.[14] We have repeated it for the consolation of all those who have like ambitions. They sometimes forget that our poor human nature has its limits, and we should not be vexed with ourselves if, in spite of our ambitions, we cannot exceed the limits of human nature.

---

[14] Charles du Bos: *Extraits d'un Journal*, 1908-1929. Ed. Correa, 1931, p. 402.

III

Good Use of Time

In the use of time, we can sin in two ways: by excessive economy and by untimely prodigality. On the one hand, there is the obsession of saving time; on the other hand, there is the triumph of time lost.

In whatever domain it may be, *to lose time unprofitably* is a folly. It is rare wisdom to know how *to lose it profitably*.

The obsession of saving time

We cite as an example a forbidding sign placed at the door of a man of letters who was always very occupied and yet produced very little: "My time is as precious as yours"; and also: "If you like to waste time, consider that of others."

In the office of a great manufacturer in Chicago, one can read on a large poster the following notice:

Visitors, be brief, my time is precious, and I will answer in advance all your useless questions:

"Am I in good health?" – "Yes, thank you."
"Isn't the weather fine?" – "That does not interest me."
"It's hot (or cold) isn't it?" – "I do not care to know."
"Have I read the newspaper?" – "I read only about the stock exchange and business."
"Is my family well?" – "I am a bachelor."
"Goodbye" – "Goodbye."

Very American, we may say. From Madame du Deffand, a true French lady of two centuries ago, we quote the following: "Those who come to see me do me honor; those who do not come do me a favor."

These statements are so exaggerated that they may have little meaning in the end. However, these exaggerations result in the killing of all friendly relations and of all those pleasant conversations in which we say nothing but in which we learn so many things. In seeking only the useful, do we not risk losing what serves life more than the useful? And, more importantly, do we not risk being guilty of a breach of the most elementary laws of propriety

Good Use of Time

with regard to the living, or even with regard to the dead? Does not the author of the *Conseils d'un American à un jeune Français*—a book in which are found some pungent observations, several of which should be noted—reproach the dead for killing the living by demanding of us, in the midst of our daily occupations, to assist at their wakes and funerals? In that passage, he goes altogether too far.

Proper decorum

Once reservations imposed by good sense, sound religious practice, or proper decorum have been established, can we not resolutely fall into step with those who want to free our life from the burden of artificial visits, which have neither charm nor purpose but are purely formal and equally unbearable for the one who makes them and for the one who receives them? Can we not free ourselves from the exchanges of trivial letters, concerning which the sole net profit is to enrich the Treasury and the Post Office, and from all the arbitrary social demands invented by people who do not know the real value of time?

Society, someone will say, is entirely built on these conventional lies to which we all more or less consent. Is it so useful that we must be obstinately set upon perpetuating this lie? We do not think so. You say that there is a friendly politeness at the base of true charity. Very well; there will never be too much of it. But do we want an ice-cold formalism that is at the base of empty worldly obligations? No, thank you! If we do not hesitate to take from our most precious time two or three hours to console a person in suffering or to nurse a sick person, that is well and good. If we take time—that which is so astonishingly extraordinary and prolific—to go, while suffering from ennui, to relate some trifles to someone whom they will really annoy, indeed, what good is done?

If we are not on guard in this respect, nothing can paralyze useful activity more than this waste of time. If only life were longer! When will one be able to work, to be recollected, if persistent people or intolerable conventions consume the best or a large part of the leisure that, fraught with silence, renders our lives fruitful?

Whoever desires to have genuinely *productive* results must know how *not to waste his time*.

When Charles Péguy was eight years old, one day, during a carnival, a parade featuring the prize ox was passing noisily beneath his window. He had climbed upon a little bench, and as he stood there, he drew a pretty map. When asked to come and look at the street parade, he said, "I shall not move. I do not have too much time to make my

Good Use of Time

map of France." Does one not see already in this childish trait the man who later could declare without telling a lie, "I have always taken everything seriously"?

The Charles Péguys are rare! We are not speaking of talent but of that solicitude for saving time. During the days of youth, we imagine that we will always have leisure. We stroll about; we muse upon things. It is not a question here of the strolling about in the manner of *La Fontaine*. From that, masterpieces are begotten. Here, it is a question of real loafing, caused by laziness and inertia. In his rule of life, Msgr. de Ségur had written as a very young abbot, "Regular work; beware of ease. I must not fritter away time in my room."

Some people can waste their time royally with a great deal of success. They will never succeed in anything. "I owe all my success in life," wrote Nelson, "to the fact that I have always and in everything been a quarter of an hour ahead of time." A true formula for being victorious at Trafalgar?

Donoso Cortes, the Spanish ambassador to France, reproached himself for the way he used his time: "When God will judge me, I shall have to answer Him only this, 'I paid visits.'" Moreover, did the visits paid by him relate to the duties of his position? If they understood the duty of their position and that of others, many men would give up two-thirds of their "friendly visits."

Uncommon Virtue

Fr. Lancicius, of whom we have already spoken, was a very hard worker. He disliked wasting his time so much that it seems as if to reward him, God granted him this favor: every time that he had to look up an item, a text, or reference, the book would open of its own accord at the desired place.

Most men do not merit a similar favor. We are obliged to use our own resources. However, for the one who wishes to use them and save his time, real "miracles" are possible. The Jesuit Fr. Petau used his leisure moments to make a translation of the Psalms into Greek verse. It is related of Aguesseau that his dinner was often not ready on time. As a result, the illustrious chancellor one day presented to his wife in the way of an *hors d'oeuvre* a volume written by him during the fifteen-minute periods he had to wait before sitting down at the table.

These are amusing incidents, but here are more serious ones.

Doumer, who started out with nothing and rose to high places in life, furnishes a characteristic example of success won by strenuous work. As a minor employee, he finished his work for a bachelor's degree. Then came the master of arts degree, and we know the rest.[15]

[15] Paul Doumer (1857–1932) was born into a working class family and earned a bachelor's degree after taking

Good Use of Time

Ramsay MacDonald and Lloyd George, both English prime ministers, were also constant workers. As a boy, Lloyd George loved to read about Napoleon, admired his legendary resistance to intellectual fatigue, and sought to be his rival in endurance. Not everything is up to chance. Work, strenuous work, now and then, helps chance. Louis XIV, Lyautey, and Poincaré[16]—we purposely associate the most dissimilar characters—were also energetic workers.[17]

> evening courses at the Conservatoire de Arts et Metiers. He later worked as a middle school teacher for two years, during which time he worked to receive a law degree. Doumer went on to become involved in politics and foreign relations, serving in such positions as Minister of Finance, Governor-General of Indochina, Senator of Corsica, President of the Senate, and finally, president of the Republic of France from June 1931 until his tragic assassination in May 1932.
>
> [16] The reign of King Louis XIV (1638-1715) was defined by an absolute monarchy, and under him, France became the leading power in Europe. Hubert Lyautey (1854-1934), "the French Empire Builder," was a general in the French Army and a Marshal of France. Raymond Poincaré (1860-1934) was the President of France from 1913-1920 and also served three terms as the Prime Minister of France.
>
> [17] Ramsay MacDonald (1866-1937) was the first Prime Minister of the United Kingdom from the Labour Party. Lloyd George (1863-1945) was the last Liberal Party politician to hold the office of Prime Minister.

Uncommon Virtue

Recounting Louis XIV, one of his historians tells us that as a young man, he worked fourteen hours a day at his official business as king, and that fifty-four years later, he worked even longer.[18] Retiring at eleven o'clock at night, and back at his office again at seven o'clock in the morning, Raymond Poincaré worked all day with a method that served a rare intelligence and an astounding memory. When he was president of the Republic, he went one day from Paris to Sampigny in an automobile. The car was driven very fast, and this caused many jolts. "This is the last time that I will take it," he declared, "I have not been able to work for one moment." "Did you expect to work?" "I never wasted five hours like this in my whole life!"

Few persons have more persevering workers than the Bolshevist leaders. During the twenty or thirty years which they used to prepare their *coup d'état*, they tried to save every minute. They were truly terrific workers before they became the leaders we know them to be. "Never," writes one of their historians,[19] "would the Bolshevists have been

[18] J. Boulenger, *Le Grand Siécle*, p. 178.
[19] Serge Popoff, *Sous l'Étoile des Soviets* (Paris: Plon), pp. 177–179.

able to accomplish the feat necessary to attain power and maintain it if they had been simple rioters, brigands, and revolutionaries and not remarkable scholars and intellectual heroes as well. They worked day and night."

The majority of the Bolshevist leaders remained on duty fourteen to sixteen hours on an average day, especially at the beginning of their struggle. Tchitcherin even had a small bed installed in his office and worked from five o'clock in the evening till eleven o'clock in the morning.[20] It is believed that this was the cause of his extreme nervousness. The illness from which Lenin suffered at the end of his life can be explained by the excess of his intense work.

Necessary relaxation

This is exactly why the counsel "to know how not to lose time" must be corrected by the counsel "to know how to lose time," or in other words, to acquire the difficult art—difficult for him who possesses a great enthusiasm for work—of knowing how to rest when necessary.

[20] Georgy Vasilyevich Chicherin (1872–1936), also spelled Tchitcherin, was a Russian Marxist leader and a Soviet politician.

Uncommon Virtue

"The sin of overworking," as it has been called, is a sin frequently committed. Those who work often work too much, or rather, they often work badly, feverishly, and without the necessary relaxation.

For several years, there was in France a humorist, or wit, who at every change of ministry sent to the interior offices his plan for increasing the country's economic efficiency. This citizen, a careful statistician, had calculated that every day all of us lose at least on an average a full hour and a half by walking too slowly. If we could recover it, this hour and a half would permit an increase of work from which our social life would benefit. But at what pace should one walk? This good man fixed it at the official rhythm of light infantry. Of course, exceptions would be made for children and those leading them, for old people, and for the sick. Women, he felt sure, would be the first to give an example of this sprightly step. This citizen, the great traffic master, sent a statement of ideas of reform to each new minister.

Perhaps he was a fool, or perhaps he was a wise man! Let us leave him the benefit of his discovery. Life is already filled with enough excitement. If it is necessary, moreover, to double or increase ten times our pace, what a wild dance our days will be! But that is not the secret of our fruitful

Good Use of Time

existence. It would be far more expedient to slacken our pace and allow ourselves a sensible speed. These are conditions necessary for productive labor.

"We have all known people who from early dawn threw themselves into the rush of business. They went along all day in a kind of blind and buzzing rage. If it happened that they were alone for a moment, they drew out their notebooks and jotted down a few notes.... To see these wretched beings who were formerly powerful personalities, one would think that their souls were poor and infirm relatives relegated to an interior region with which they never concerned themselves."

Thus speaks Georges Duhamel in *La Possession du Monde* (Possession of the World), an interesting title! These busy people will never be "those who possess the land." The author continues:

"Some people have told me: 'My happiness is that very hurly-burly, that beastly labor, that mad excitement which you spurn. Outside of that turmoil of business and of society, I am bored. I need it in order to divert my mind.' Without doubt, without doubt! But what have you done with your life that it becomes necessary for you to divert yourself? What have you done with your past, what do you expect from your future, that this alcohol and this opium are necessary for you?"[21]

Before the author of *La Possession du Monde* had written those words, another writer, Henri-Frederic Amiel, had already said:

> Yes, we are too full of business, too encumbered, too occupied, too active! We read too much! We must know how to throw overboard all our impediments of anxieties and preoccupations. Yes, we must know how to be *idle* in a way which is not the result of laziness. By attentive and recollected inactivity, our soul wipes away its wrinkles. It relaxes, unfolds, is reborn softly as the tramped-on grass of the pathway, and, like rain in the night, it revives the ideas worn out and grown dim by the heat of the day. Being mild and fruitful, it awakens in us a thousand sleeping ideas. While enjoying itself, it accumulates material for the future and the imagery for the use of talent. Reverie is the Sunday of thought, and who knows whether the laborious tension of the week or the vivifying repose of the

---

[21] Georges Duhamel, *La Possession du Monde* (Paris: Mercure de France), pp. 30 and 35.

Good Use of Time

Sabbath may be the more important for man and the more beneficial.[22]

Let us leave the profane world. History tells us that St. Teresa of the Infant Jesus loved this passage of the *Imitation*: "Let those who are agitated, be agitated; as for thee, remain thou in peace!" To a novice who threw herself with too much ardor into her work, she recommended composure: "You torment yourself too much concerning your work. You ought to be detached from yourself and your personal work and employ conscientiously therein the time prescribed, but with disengagement of heart."[23]

The great master of retreats for priests, Fr. Chaignon, who handled a great deal of work and increased his ministrations to the point that he did not allow himself a minute to breathe, once received a letter from his general, the Rev. Fr. Roothaan, who wrote to tell him to be more moderate and to grant himself some leisure. Wasted effort! The apostle, who is a tireless worker, rests eight hours and begins again. Moreover, after a certain time, it becomes impossible for him to rest. Not to be working causes him

---

[22] H.-F. Amiel, *Journal intime*, I, pp. 52-53.
[23] Pere Petitot, O.P., *Sainte Thérèse de l'Enfant-Jésus*, pp. 136-137.

greater fatigue than the most tiring work. In general, that pays. However, not everybody is able to prolong this urge to work as Fr. Chaignon did, even to the age of ninety-two!

Another Jesuit, Fr. de Clorivière, companion to his Provincial for some years before the Revolution, never granted himself, so to say, any rest. His principal historian tells us that he continued in this way beyond his duty and almost beyond discretion. In his spiritual diary for 1768, he wrote, "Today I have wasted some time in turning over the leaves of a book, partly out of curiosity." A few days later he noted, "I have wasted nearly an hour perusing hastily a book, through curiosity rather than through a serious motive." He kept such a vigorous and efficacious watch over himself that the following year, he could write at the time of his retreat, "I cannot find that I have wasted time with regard to anything."

It is seen that he reproached himself particularly for certain reading. For those who devote themselves to mental work, reading can be one of the most habitual forms of laziness. How many people forbid themselves to think, to reflect, to compose—to work hard or to produce something, in whatever field it might be—because they find a journal, a magazine, or sometimes, but more rarely, a book, and they do not resist the temptation to take it and spend their time with it, quite often without much profit. They have the illusion of being occupied. Occupation is the counterpoint of real work. There are many people who are occupied and even busy, but there are few persons who really work, that is, produce. This in turn means to put their soul, or something of their soul, energetically and, if possible, powerfully into the activity which their duty assigns them.

An occupation is only work to the extent that it requires a greater or lesser amount of reflection.

Happy are those who lose time in order to reflect. They are the true conquerors of life. The world belongs to them. The rest are merely day laborers.

The following spiritual passage in one of the works of Emile Augier is familiar:

> Let us never speak ill of leisure,
> The sweetest and the best-known thing in life.
> Busy people give me the impression of those misers
> Who always complain that their dollars are few,
> And who lend them instead of using them,
> Until death comes to take them away from them.
> Life is short! Well! Let us not give an hour
> To anything which is not an interior joy;
> Let us take a walk along the brook, under the sky,

With some loved ones. That is the essential thing.[24]

Conclusion

We must know how to work, that is to say, above all, to reflect. In order to rest, we must know how to make a truce with reflection and to occupy ourselves by a loving association with others, whether books or persons. That is the ideal.

Like every ideal, it is a limit toward which one can aspire; to hope ever to attain it, at least completely, is impossible. For a long time, the lives of those who seek to work will be burdened by conventions or by troublesome persons. That is their most efficacious purgatory. For a long time, too, the throng of the occupied will imagine that they are working.

People will continue for a long time to waste a great deal of time and not know how to rest successfully, or perhaps we should say "seriously." From this results the excessive passion for amusement and distraction and the relative scarcity of truly masterful productions.

---

[24] E. Augier, *Philiberte*, Act II, sc. v, words of Philiberte.

IV

The Spirit of Discretion

We can be indiscreet in many ways: by spreading out excessively and in such a manner as to occupy a whole place or too much place; by meddling in affairs about which we have not been consulted; by seeking to know the secrets of others; by taking advantage of the kindness of others; by not knowing how to remain within the bounds that a given situation demands; in other words by pretension, indelicacy, curiosity, lack of tact, or lack of moderation.

We shall speak here of the spirit of discretion or moderation. Again, this will not be on secular grounds but in the spiritual domain.

Ne quid nimis: avoid excess, exaggeration. By discretion, we mean that practical wisdom by which we find spontaneously in each circumstance what is fitting to say, what to do or not to do. In a more special way, discretion is that moral aptitude for not going to excess in the practice of virtues; to adhere, not to a common level, but to a level of a generosity, which, in order to be ardent, does not cease to be well-balanced. Discretion is so necessary a virtue that St. Bernard used to say to his novices, "Wherever it does not reside, virtue itself becomes a vice, good becomes bad."[25]

As a simply human quality

Considered simply as a human quality, discretion is precious. Born of an innate tendency or of a good training, it maintains a prudent reserve, causes certain intemperate acts to be avoided, hinders inopportune and excessive haste, and guards against blunders. With regard to your neighbor, it renders life agreeable. Nothing is more annoying than having to submit to troublesome persons who come and take advantage of your time or of your readiness to oblige them. Not one has the audacity to defend his door with the help of pointed signs or to reply as wittily as Rossini did to a person who, after having asked his advice

[25] *"Tolle hanc et virtus vitium erit."* Vacandard, *Vie de saint Bernard*, I, 493. As to the use of the means in reaching sanctity, St. Thomas Aquinas makes moderation a part of the virtue of prudence. See *Summa Theologica*, II-II, Q. 49, art. 7-8.

on two of his musical productions, presented himself a second time. "Ah! Yes, your two attempts? I have had time only to read the first." "What do you think of it?" "I prefer the other."[26]

People who are always boasting about themselves, as if there were no one but themselves in the world, are also very disagreeable. It is better to please than to boast, as Joubert has so well said. Scholars, eminent statesmen, artists, and men of letters do not render themselves a good service by making a display of the least details of their private lives. No man is great in the eyes of his valet. As a rule, we become less esteemed through too much intimacy. Claude Bernard[27] was right when he noted in his *Cahier Rouge*: "Today, authors admit us to their rise, or sneeze.... That is a false point of view. A man is great not when he rises, lies down, or sneezes; he is great when he writes and when he thinks. In those moments, man is truly great, and we know him by his works. It is better

---

[26] Noel Desjoyauz, *Figures de Musiciens*, R. D. M. January 1, 1944, p. 86.

[27] Claude Bernard (1813–1878) was a French physiologist and one of the founders of modern experimental medicine. The *Cahier Rouge* is Bernard's laboratory notebook, in which he writes of his experiments as well as his experiences as an experimental physiologist.

not to know the rest. That does not add anything to the man, that can only belittle him."[28]

In the moral domain

In the moral domain, we must first of all guard against confusing discretion with mediocrity. Under pretense of avoiding excess, are we constrained to avoid enthusiasm? Consider such words as those of St. Bernard: "The measure of loving God is to love Him without measure"; or those of St. Bonaventure: "The fervor of novices must have a horror for indulgent self-pity."[29] Can we ever give too much to the Lord? Is not God a consuming fire, as is said in Deuteronomy?[30] We look at the saints; they vie with one another in zeal for the folly of the Cross. Is not the world dying from using too much discretion, and is Christianity not running the risk of becoming degenerate? Men who write of religious activities are not pleased to note that in general, our baptized people are not outstanding for the excess of their zeal. Long ago, Montesquieu had a casuist answer for his Persian neighbor: "Except for

[28] (Gallimard), *Introduction*.
[29] *Fervorem novitiorum non decent illae misericordes in seipsis discretiones.*
[30] 4:24.

The Spirit of Discretion

a few freethinkers, all Christians want to earn Heaven; but there is no one who does not want to earn it as cheaply as possible." Is this what Christ came to teach us: a religion without demands, loyalty at a reduced price?

Not at all! The Gospel is above all the law of love, and the religion of Jesus Christ is a religion of the greatest generosity.

But with the exception of a few points strictly demanded of all, there are different degrees of fervor to be attained. Not everyone is obliged to enter upon the way of the counsels,[31] and for those who follow the way of the simple commandments, there is no single standard. Some will communicate every month; others every day. One man will say just a short prayer every evening; another will devote a half hour or an hour to prayer. Even those who practice the vows of poverty, chastity, and obedience or live in the priesthood do not necessarily have the same spiritual enlightenment in order to reach the ideal to which they have consecrated themselves.

Aspirations or practices are indiscreet when they are not in conformity with the graces bestowed and with one's

---

[31] The three evangelical counsels are chastity, poverty, and obedience. These counsels developed into the monastic vows made by those who devote themselves to the consecrated life.

Uncommon Virtue

vocation in life. For each person, the essential thing is to use every grace granted to him and to practice the sanctity demanded of him. "I say ... to all that are among you," St. Paul wrote to the Romans, "not to be more wise than it behoveth to be wise, but to be wise unto sobriety: and according as God hath divided to every one the measure of faith" (12:3).

In general, we must acknowledge that we sin chiefly through cowardice. But there are some excessive temperaments, some inexperienced souls who have more courage sometimes than wise discernment. It is here that the virtue of discretion has a distinct place. In that sense, indiscretion is a risk for generous hearts. They burn with an ardent love and are tempted not to take account of their strength, be it physical strength or moral endurance. For such souls, direction is important. Its role is not to stimulate but to enlighten, to slacken, and to moderate.

There can be excessive eagerness, a confusion between sensible ardor and genuine zeal, between fervor and effervescence, with the risk of setting the goal too high, of taking resolutions which, in practice, will not hold good. This is not because cowardice intervenes but because, objectively, the proposed program overburdens a person's powers. He has forgotten that he cannot do everything

The Spirit of Discretion

in a few minutes and that it is necessary to understand clearly the well-known aphorism, "To be a saint, it suffices to will it." Yes, we must be like Fr. de Ravignan,[32] who learned to will his sanctity not only for an hour or a day but continually, for a lifetime. It is slowly and by degrees that a virtue is acquired, and each advance, be it ever so small, costs a great deal.

"Make haste slowly and without losing courage." This is much more true when we are training ourselves in virtue than when we are training ourselves in good diction or poetry.

Again, there can be indiscretion because a secret vanity inclines us to be immoderate, or because ignorance of what true virtue is misleads us.

When Fr. d'Alzon[33] founded the Order of the Assumption, he entrusted to Fr. Pernet the responsibility of examining the vocation of a young converted Jew who had come to offer himself to the newly founded Institute but who seemed to him animated by an immature enthusiasm: "I want to go to shed my blood in a pagan

---

[32] Fr. Gustave Delacroix de Ravignan (1795–1858), called the "Apostle of Paris," was a Jesuit preacher and author in France.

[33] Fr. Emmanuel d'Alzon (1810–1880).

land as soon as possible," confided this excellent youth to Fr. Pernet. The priest answered him, "First, learn how to clean vegetables, how to cook, and how to sweep the corridors. Moreover, in order to preach the Faith, it is necessary to know it and to study it." The young man said, "Is it not sufficient for me to know that Christ came to preach it?" And putting his hand to his forehead, he continued, "Do you not see there the Blood of Christ which has fallen on my head?" To this, Fr. Pernet answered, "My friend, I do not see anything, except that you are bald. Moreover, you have been baptized. The Blood of mercy has removed the blood of malediction. Let us put aside all declamation. Let us speak in a very simple, calm, and clear prose. Prudence and simplicity. Prudence consists in obeying, and simplicity is common sense, real common sense."[34]

If, in accordance with wisdom, and never without asking for prudent advice, we believe ourselves able to do that which exceeds the common standard, it will yet be necessary to guard against flaunting our virtue at the risk of humiliating our neighbor. In the time of the desert fathers, St. Macarius gave this counsel: "If there is wine,

---

[34] Gaétan Bernoville, *Vie du P. Pernet*, Grasset, p. 53.

The Spirit of Discretion

drink wine for the sake of your brethren; but for each glass of wine you must not drink for one day. In other words: When you are in the company of others, do as everyone does; as to your penance, God alone should be witness to it." That is in harmony with what our Savior said: "When you fast, be not as the hypocrites, sad. For they disfigure their faces, that they may appear unto men to fast.... But thou, when thou fastest anoint thy head, and wash thy face; that thou appear not fasting to men, but to thy Father who is in secret: and thy Father who seeth in secret, will repay thee" (Matt. 6:16-18).

Sometimes, indiscretion has its source in a secret inspiration of the evil spirit. He will prompt excessive acts which he will cash in later. At a time of weariness, he will prompt acts of cowardice which will risk compromising a vocation. He will incline souls toward inconsiderate and untimely reading, such as the reading of mystic authors when an asceticism more to their level is probably indicated. Under the pretense of exalted prayers, one man may neglect the duty of our state. Under pretense of mortification, another may go beyond the permission of obedience. We remember the incident which happened unexpectedly to St. Margaret Mary. Once, when she was taking the discipline and was carried away by her zeal for the deliverance of the souls in Purgatory, she exceeded the number of blows agreed upon by the superior. "Up to this point, it was proper for us," she heard an interior voice saying to her, "from now on, it is no longer for us."

St. John Climacus tells us of having been witness of certain cases of fervor which, if not positively indiscreet, were at least so singular that the demon could easily have taken advantage of them. A monk who was shamefully treated rejoices over it heartily. Out of humility, he begins to weep and lament in order to make himself be misjudged. Another acknowledges himself altogether unworthy of the first places but feigns to desire them. There are better examples. A hermit to whom some raisins were given pounces upon them in order to simulate gluttony. Another, having lost some figs, shows himself voluntarily distressed over it throughout the day. Both acted in this way in order to deceive the demon. The saint, without condemning such actions, notes with a good deal of common sense, "Those who wish to act in this manner must use on these occasions a great circumspection, lest by wishing to trick the demons, they become their playthings."[35]

---

[35] J. P. Migne, *Patrologia Graeca*, 88, 1.064. Cited by J. Bremond, *Les Peres du Desert* (Paris: Gabalda), pp. 127–128.

The Spirit of Discretion

The work of God is a work of order and of wisdom. The demon finds his opportunity by putting wisdom aside and by disturbing order. When it is a question of ordinary souls, he uses ordinary means, attracting these souls most frequently to worthless objects. With generous souls, he uses means which appear to be of the highest merit. Skillful in transforming himself into an angel of light, in the same way as St. Ignatius notes very precisely in his *Rules for the Discernment of Spirits*, he will suggest devotions, penances, and aspirations which seem praiseworthy at first sight but have no other aim than to turn a man away from his duty, to weaken him physically or morally, to discourage him in the face of untimely or excessive effort, and to cast him into a state of illusion or vanity.

Pope Pius IX once asked Fr. Passaglia, a professor of theology at the Gregorian University in Rome, to prepare the material which should serve to compose the bull in honor of the Immaculate Conception. By his competence and his work, he was among the best qualified. Later on, thinking that he was giving more glory to God by studying theology than by fulfilling his exercises of rule, he had come to omit his hour of daily prayer. Little by little, his religious fervor decreased; and so one fine day, he asked for his dispensation papers and left his community. The demon had attained his ends.

Uncommon Virtue

Indiscretion can also have for its cause too great a confidence in our own intellect. We refer only to our own personal judgment when it would be wise to consult an experienced guide. Without doubt, there is such a thing as generosity of spirit, but there is also presumption. It is more prudent and more humble to be enlightened before making resolutions. One man will lay down for himself a rule of life that is too crowded; another will impose upon himself so many practices that it is impossible to continue them for any considerable time. Still another will create for himself a schedule of work that lacks a proper balance, or a program of penance that is not to the purpose.

Danger of indiscreet fervor

Whatever may be its cause, indiscreet fervor has the following evil consequences. These are at least the principal ones.

First, it exhausts the soul and runs the risk of carrying off that real courage which is needed for the small and humble tasks of everyday life, for putting into practice resolutions less lofty but more continually demanded. In every field, it is a recognized principle that *violentum non durat*: a violent effort cannot continue for a long time. The old Romans, with a wisdom at

The Spirit of Discretion

times slightly dull but solid, counselled, *sutor ne ultra crepidam*: let the cobbler stick to shoes.

In the second place, indiscreet fervor runs the risk of irritating one's neighbors. It is not by shouting to his servant, "Laurent, lock up my haircloth and scourge," that Tartuffe[36] makes evangelical mortification loved. He makes light of what we have, and not without reason, because of some whim, some importunity, or some exaggeration. As greatly as intelligent, vigorous, and sustained Christian practice gains sympathy and leads souls to Christ, so much does the abuse of devotions, the multiplication of pious works, and the crowding together of exercises disaffect not only the negligent but even those who are animated by a genuine fervor.

The third evil consequence of indiscretion in piety and the exercise of virtues is that it deforms true religion and makes God ridiculous. Our Savior did not come from Heaven to bring us a religion of additional burdens and of excessive practices. Above all, faith is life. It is to be marked not only by an adherence of the spirit but also by acts. There is nothing more certain than this. But it is fitting that the manifestations, especially the exterior

---

[36] *Tartuffe* is a comedic play written by Molière.

ones, of our faith be in conformity with doctrine and with the teaching of the Church, which almost equally loves generosity, moderation, prudence, and proper balance.

But the excess of the saints?

If, in the history of Christianity, there have been examples of fervor which seem excessive to us, it is fitting to remark here:

First, what is permitted to the saints is not advisable for all. At the beginning of a sermon on St. Clare of Assisi, Fr. Binet, a seventeenth-century Jesuit, said not without humor to his audience: "Beware of imitating our saint; it will be quite sufficient for you to admire her." God may suggest to certain very superior souls generosities beyond comparison. For them, it is not indiscretion. They are at the height of the virtues which the Lord has inspired, while for us, there would be a notorious disproportion with our capacities. Let us admire them, indeed. Let us thank God for these proofs of a love which transcends the earth, and let us blush at our realizations, more modest often than is fitting, but let us not seek to acquire a form of virtue which is out of our reach.

If God permits these examples, it is for the honor of His Gospel and the glory of His divine Son. A religion in

The Spirit of Discretion

which there is no place for heroism would not be worthy of His sovereign grandeur, but we cannot conclude from this that all are dedicated to heroism.

Moreover, where it is a question of generosity according to God, pious excesses, or those which appear such, are accompanied by two marks that enable us to judge them at their true value, instead of describing them as indiscreet.

The first mark is this: The practices in question, which with everyone else would rightly be called excessive, form the part of a synthesis of virtues that assures them a solid foundation. It is not a matter of a solitary peak emerging from a drab existence that is level with the ground or of a summit which astonishes one because nothing prepares its emergence. It is a matter of a continuous chain of considerable elevations. We are not amazed that here or there a more lofty peak rises. The generosities of everyday life account for and support generosity in the highest degree.

Even where there is seemingly misdirected fervor, we can expect, if the inspiration comes really from God, to find a sign of prudence which asserts itself in spite of everything.

If there is a life in which excess seems to be the rule, it is indeed the life of Fr. William Doyle, an Irish chaplain in World War I. Fr. Doyle spent nights at the front in prayer, imposed upon himself austere mortifications, put himself under the obligation of turning to God almost incessantly, and bound himself by a vow under pain of mortal sin not to refuse any sacrifice which he would clearly see to be demanded of him by our Lord.[37] But never did he do anything without the direction of his spiritual directors and under their guidance. Next, listen to him speak to others. You will find no trace of excess, but on the contrary, the wisest prudence.

"I firmly believe in corporal penance, but it is a means to an end."

"And what looks like frenzy ought to be suspected by you and not to be accepted."

"While urging you to be generous, I desire at the same time that you remain sensible. Remember these two rules: (1) If, after an honest effort, you find that a certain practice really fatigues you or interferes with your work, abandon it. (2) Be on your guard so that your body may not be overworked and the spirit suffer from it, as the prudent St. Ignatius said. The same thing is not good for all."

[37] Alfred O'Rahilly, *Father William Doyle*, 5th ed. (New York: Longmans, Green, 1940). See also the article by Fr. de Grandmaison in the *Revue d'Ascetique et de Mystique*, April 1921.

The Spirit of Discretion

The extraordinary fervor of some souls is explained by the following reason. As there are too many Christians who have no fervor, God permits by way of compensation some fervors to transcend the average. When we think of all the sins, all the neglect in the obedience to duty, and all the cowardice to be atoned for, we understand why certain souls may have aspired to the folly of the Cross. The worldly-minded are astonished to see the Church canonize in the person of the mendicant Benedict Labre a saint who had let himself be devoured by vermin. In his cathedral at Poitiers, Msgr. Pie did not hesitate to offer this triumphant interpretation: "Vermin for vermin, better is the vermin of the body than that of the soul!" The reason is here a common one, a social one: to check the forces of sin. But not everybody is called to be a Trappist or to become a Charles de Foucauld.[38]

Furthermore, in cases of true sanctity, even where virtue greatly exceeds the ordinary level, we find a simple goodness of heart and a sweetness that are not found in

---

[38] Blessed Charles Eugène de Foucauld (1858–1916, beatified November 13, 2005) was a French priest and missionary who was martyred in Algeria. The Congregation for the Causes of Saints has declared that Bl. Foucald will be canonized a saint on May 15, 2022.

indiscreet fervor or in a fervor that has not reached its full degree of maturity. A point to be observed is that the Church accepts the presentation of a cause for beatification only if it is a case of a person who has practiced virtue not only for a notable length of time and under unusual circumstances but also in a serene way, without excessive vigor and without feverish agitation. So much does she insist, even in the midst of excessive charity, on not finding anything which indicates excess.

V

Facing Life

Courage

There are two great forms of courage: one consists in *doing*, the other consists in *suffering*. Which of the two is the more meritorious?

At war, in regiments and battalions, the men discuss their preference. Which is better: to seize a position by assault, or to organize and hold a position already taken?

Honor surely belongs to those who run toward danger. Honor also belongs to those who, without running toward it, do not fear it when it threatens to fall upon them at every moment. The first form of courage has more outward glory, and for that reason, it is perhaps easier. The second form is more humble. It does not imply less bravery but a bravery of another quality. To rush forth is magnificent; to run into

Uncommon Virtue

danger in spite of the trembling due to sensibility, or the hesitations suggested by reason of some hidden cowardice, is courage. For courage is "the art of being afraid without showing it," and it is to act as if one were brave in spite of interior protests. But to persevere in trial, especially when the trial lasts and when its burden each day becomes heavier, shows another valor.

To persevere in spite of the time that stretches out endlessly, in spite of increasing privations, in spite of conditions that grow worse, the deepening perplexities, and an uncertain tomorrow; to persevere in trusting the call of one's country, not because we think that it cannot be saved without our effort but in order to encourage ourselves and to give all our strength to the common cause; to persevere in order that our example may fortify our neighbor; to persevere not with empty talk but with determination; to persevere without letting ourselves be deceived by news that flatters our hopes too much; to persevere even if the darkest night and the most frightful storms come upon us; to persevere up to the moment when the dawn will break.

Here is a letter written by an officer to his young wife in 1939 at the beginning of World War II, a man who would later be killed while defending his retreating division. On September 13, 1939, he wrote: "Let us be frank: the thought of the sacrifice which it may be necessary to make for the welfare and peace of humanity has not been a source of joy. I cannot hide from you that I have had some periods, fortunately short, in which thoughts of discouragement have assailed me." We see that the captain wishes neither to boast nor to profess sentiments that he does not feel. He is loyal; he is humble. Then, having reflected and prayed better, he can add: "Now with the help of God, whom I, like you, have the happiness to receive every day, the sacrifice is accepted in its entirety. Its different aspects have been presented to me. I have looked at them squarely, and with God's grace, I am no longer afraid."

What is to be said of such words? As long as there spring from the soil men capable of speaking thus, of feeling thus, and of sacrificing themselves thus, we must feel ourselves animated with loftier hopes. Beyond doubt, there is here an instance of a chosen soul. But in our times, should not all souls be chosen souls or become such?

We must not force our strength, and we must not consider ourselves more brave and more capable of endurance than we are. Let us examine our conscience: if we are still cowards, we should be willing to acknowledge it. "The thought of the sacrifice has not been a source of joy." We must not consent to remain at that stage. We must understand the great interests that are at stake, what our country demands of us, and what God asks of us. If we have faith, let us pray; for in order to accept the sacrifice, grace is necessary and grace is bought. Let us ask it for those who do not have the good fortune to believe or who have only a tepid faith.

May all succeed in being able to render themselves the beautiful words: "The sacrifice is accepted in its entirety. ... I have looked at them squarely, and with God's grace, I am no longer afraid."

To proceed slowly

The Italian adage *chi va piano va sano*, "to go slowly is to go safely," displeased the great Marshal Lyautey.

It was not that he despised a sensible slowness, but it was slowness for the sake of slowness and as possessing a virtue in itself that exasperated the man whose motto was "Act, act, act." He did not add: "To act as quickly as the situation permits," but that was included in the action which accompanied his resolution.

He had a grudge against certain French proverbs which seem to preach the least effort: "A rolling stone gathers no moss," the condemnation of those who wish to travel over the wide world in order to enrich their experience;

Facing Life

"Patience brings all things about," when on the contrary, it is much more necessary to go ahead of circumstances than to wait and see; "It is no good hurrying, you must start punctually," which, he said, is more frequently an excuse not for leaving on time but for not running! For him, the most deadly adage of all was: "Let well enough alone." He condemned it as abominable, as the negation of all progress and the excuse for all inertia. This fatal proverb had been held up to him when he asked from the public officials a quick solution of an urgent case, and when it was delayed by the roundabout ways of endless or obsolete formalities.

Wherever they may be, and to whatever career they may belong, all great souls reason in the same way. Gosset, the eminent surgeon, used to speak of his patron, Prof. Terrier, and his way of proceeding by following his example. Many times, he found himself facing distressing problems, extremely difficult cases in which were needed both discernment and the spirit of initiative and daring. At such moments, he asked himself: "What would Terrier, my teacher, have done?"

"The question having been stated, I no longer hesitated. I knew in a most clear way that in doubt he would not have refrained from acting; that in a hopeless case where there only were one chance in a million, this chance he would have taken; that in the face of a grave responsibility, even if there had been an honorable way of fleeing from it, he would not have attempted it; and finally, that once having suffered a defeat or a blow, he never complained and accepted all the consequences, whatever they were."[39]

Similarly, we too meet with a compact philosophy like this. We hear it expressed every day, or we find many instances of it on life's paths. Well and good! Instead of harping on some trite slogans, good at most when one breaks an arm or a leg, instead of lamenting, sighing, or seeking sympathy and palliative advice, would we not all gain by expressing only elevating maxims, by showing invincible courage, and by preparing ourselves through daily daring in duties resolutely embraced for the hard blows and the delicate or sorrowful events which life brings?

Maintain serenity in everything

"I have had many trials in my life, but most of them never happened," a wit used to say. We suffer from three things:

First, from that which pains us objectively.

[39] Prof. Gosset, member of the Institute, *Chirurgie et Chirurgiens*, preface by G. Duhamel (Paris: Gallimard), p. 102.

Facing Life

Second, from that which is going to cause us pain and from which precedes the actual arrival of the suffering. Very often, the anticipation is more painful than the evil itself. For example, the prospect of an impending surgical operation causes us more pain than the awakening after the operation and the misery of the days that follow.

But what darkens our life by far the most is the suffering that we imagine we shall have to endure. Our wit proves himself to be a good psychologist by considering his heaviest trials to be evils which never came upon him but which he spent his time fearing. Our most cruel sufferings are our own apprehensions.

We take as an example an episode of life in the desert. Yonder, on the horizon, there is some sort of ruined building, but it scarcely can be used as an ambuscade. The traveler can move on without fear. But what are those iron-tipped lances that glitter and do not move behind that high rock? Surely some men hide there and lie in wait for the traveler in order to rob him. What is to be done? Advance? One against three is a great risk. Yet it can't be helped, come what may! And then — they prove to be only three abandoned lances.

The dangers that we see before our path are often unreal. It is enough that we must suffer in reality, without adding imaginary sufferings. What is the use of untiringly composing litanies with all this "What would happen if …"? The future is never what the present imagines. Most frequently, when it has become the present, it is less dark than we imagined. We Christians know that every case brings with it its own grace. At the passing minute, I do not have the necessary aid in order to accept such or such a moment in the future. If suddenly, tomorrow, in a year, in ten years, God demands of me a sacrifice, He will give me the grace needed to make it. He is not bound to grant that grace at present, since the trial to be endured will only come later. Grace follows the course of time. Let us live one hour at a time. Sufficient for the day is the evil thereof and the patience to endure that evil.

It is said, "We never live, we hope to live." That is proposed periodically as the third subject for the written examinations for the baccalaureate, first part. One could also quite well modify it like this: "We never suffer, we fear to suffer."

This is unfruitful, discouraging, and without efficacy.

There has perhaps been too much insistence in the course of our training, on Perrette's distress at her broken milk pitcher.[40] Much more interesting is her joyous

[40] In Jean de La Fontaine's poem "The Milkmaid and the Pot of Milk," Perrette, a milkmaid, gets so excited thinking

Facing Life

intoxication during the time which preceded her unlucky fall. Let the milk pitcher be dashed to pieces; it is only a trifle! A woman takes up another, which she fills with the same rich liquid; she places it again on her head, held very erect, and she looks into the future with a smile.

A traveler regrets that our women have not as their sisters in certain warm countries the custom of carrying their burdens on their heads. Nothing, it seems, gives a more majestic carriage. I believe it. The same thing is true especially for the mental or moral faculties. Let us advance in life fearlessly and with an upright carriage.

"At the beginning was joy." Let us not permit, whatever may come, that joy does not remain in the first position. If it is necessary for the imagination to deceive us a little, may it be in order to enrich life rather than to sadden it.

Fidelity to the duties of our state of life

The first and foremost duty of one's state of life is to sanctify oneself in the providential plan fixed by God and to do one's utmost in the line of obligatory tasks.

---

about what she will buy with the money she gets for selling her jug of milk that she leaps in the air and drops the jug, spilling the milk and ending her dreams.

Uncommon Virtue

What a man is he should be with his whole being. If a man is a doctor, he should be the best possible doctor. It he is an artisan, the best artisan in the guild. If he is a butcher, a baker, a merchant, or a lawyer, he should be the best, meaning that he should be the most conscientious butcher, the most honest and capable baker, the most experienced as well as the most upright merchant, or the most competent and most honest lawyer that can be found.

A man must not escape from his primary duty by capriciously neglecting his chief job. No one is forbidden to have a hobby and during his spare time to occupy himself with some diversion or suitable occupation. Huysmans worked at the Home Office, but he loved to devote himself to literature during his leisure hours.[41] That was an excellent thing! A mother of a family who is entirely devoted to her home, her husband, and her children can take pleasure during her moments of leisure in some uplifting reading or devote herself to an apostolate that goes beyond her family circle. There is nothing better.

---

[41] Charles-Marie-Georges Huysmans (1848–1907), who published his works under the name Joris-Karl Huysmans, was a French novelist and art critic who supported his writing through a thirty-two-year career in the French Ministry of the Interior.

Facing Life

What is condemned here is the reversing of values: putting first what is subordinate and second what is first. We should be what we are before seeking to become something else. We think of Marguerite Andoux, who around 1910 was famous for a novel of exceptional freshness, entitled *Marie-Claire*. Asked whether she read reviews of her works, she answered, "You know well that I have not the time to read the newspapers." Again, she was asked, "What are you preparing right now, Marguerite?" And she answered, "My dear, some soup for my boy."

When someone spoke to Rudyard Kipling about Pierre Loti, who was both an officer in the navy and novelist, he said, "I greatly admire Pierre Loti the novelist. But, tell me, is he a good naval officer, I mean from the professional point of view?" Kipling spoke truly, for there is a complete philosophy in his innocent but shrewd question. Rather, there is quite a theology of genuine virtue. How many people seek to sanctify themselves by their everyday duties and by those ordinary tasks which earn their daily bread! A man must sanctify himself with, in, and by the everyday duty of his state.

Since a task has been given to us to perform, we should strive to fulfill it in the best possible manner. We must work first for God, whom our activity glorifies. The Lord, the Bible tells us, placed man in paradise in order that he might labor there. The riches of the earth are buried in different places. It is for us to discover them, to make the most of them, to work them, to bring them nearer to our fellow men, and to make them produce a hundredfold.

Then, we must work for ourselves. Work is the great means of human development. The most cruel punishment that could be imposed on anyone would be to condemn him to absolute immobility and to complete nirvana. Nor must we forget the social reason for our expenditure of activity. All of us are put into a group, and we have the responsibility of helping one another. No one can be entirely self-sufficient. But if each of us has need of others, those others have need of each of us. Those who claim the right of dispensing with society, or of exploiting it without furnishing it anything in return for all its contributions, are parasites. St. Paul does not hesitate to declare that they have no right to eat (2 Thess. 3:10).

Let us work; let us work for two, for three, and then for others; and let it always be a task well done.

Heaven helps those who help themselves

The Church puts at our disposal precious means for obtaining grace. Some are joined to rites that are objective bearers of grace; these are the sacraments. Others consist in petitions that we direct to God; these are our acts of prayer.

Whether it is a question of prayer or of the sacraments, these aids are not granted to us in order to dispense us from personal action, as if God took everything upon Himself and intended to act in our place. Rather, their purpose is to contribute to the valor that is needed. Beyond doubt, it is required of us to depend upon God, to rely upon Him. It is just as certain that if we do not cooperate, divine grace will work only in a meager way. The well-known adage, "Heaven helps those who help themselves," is full of meaning. St. Ignatius of Loyola, in his characteristic way, used to say, "Do everything as if you alone were doing it; do everything as if God alone were doing it." These two statements are complementary; they are not contradictory.

There is a way of being a Pelagian[42] without knowing it: by relying upon oneself. There is also a way of professing, in practice if not in theory, a kind of pious fatalism: "It belongs to God to regulate everything; there is no need for me to have a hand in it."

[42] Pelagius and his followers thought that we can perform supernatural acts by human effort alone, without the aid of supernatural assistance. This heresy was condemned by the Church.

Uncommon Virtue

We could easily find some traces of this fatalism in the conduct of certain persons. How many Christians seem ready to welcome practices of devotion that dispense them, they believe, from putting forth any effort of their own. They wear a medal, thinking that wearing the medal in itself and without any effort for good on their part is a guarantee of fidelity. They recite a certain prayer claimed to be infallible and take for granted the quasi-mechanical effect of the prayer in question. They make a certain pilgrimage, they make a novena, they give a certain promise, and without striving to display their zeal in view of the expected result, they rely only on the exterior virtue of the pilgrimage, the novena, or the promise. At the same time, they neglect in other ways to practice the virtues that a well-ordered piety would demand.

Of course, these means are excellent and these practices are commendable; but everything depends on the spirit that guides them. Their purpose is not to render unnecessary the work of the soul. On the contrary, in the mind of the God who suggests them or of the Church which recommends them, their purpose is to stimulate powers that will enable means and practices to produce their effect.

We all know of persons who suspend a cross from their necks and yet completely neglect to carry their interior crosses. On their exterior, they place a religious symbol, as if that dispensed them in their family and in their relations with society from friendliness, devotion, and humility. They scarcely seem to suspect that the cross is not only an attractive little piece of jewelry that looks well when mounted on fine cloth but that it must be a constant spur to the spirit of penance and generosity.

When the Master gave the counsel *Orate et vigilate*, He did not separate prayer seeking help on high from personal vigilance. In order to have the complete meaning of the expression, we should perhaps interpret it: *Orate ut vigiletis:* Pray to have the courage for the vigilance that is imposed on you and for the victories that God asks of you. Prayer to obtain God's assistance, if it is not accompanied by the desire of giving Him, through personal effort, the desirable efficacy, is a profanation rather than a use of God's help.

Prayers act *ex opere operantis*,[43] that is to say, they are dependent on the virtue of the one who utters them. When it comes to the sacraments, on the other hand, it

---

[43] To be distinguished from *ex opere operato*, which refers to the built-in efficacy of a sacrament, *ex opere operantis* is a term applied to the disposition with which the sacrament is received.

may be said that they are entirely different. While interior dispositions are not the *cause* of the value of the sacrament, they are the *condition* of their greater or lesser benefit.

Consider the Eucharist: the priest places the Sacred Host on the lips of someone who is in the state of mortal sin; next on the lips of a just person; then on the lips of someone who refuses God nothing and strives for perfection with all his power. Is the effect the same in all three cases? Very far from it.

Each of these communicants in truth receives the Body of Christ. But while the first receives Him unto his perdition and commits a sacrilege that is added to his other sins, the second and the third receive Him for their benefit. Yet this is a benefit that differs in other respects. The one who is in the state of grace but shows scarcely any generosity in the service of the Lord is far from benefiting from the same advantages as he whose love of God is of the highest degree. No one will say that there is an identical effect between a Communion of the Virgin Mary and one of our Communions. It is the same Savior in both cases, but what a difference in the plenitude of the reception!

"So many Communions," we hear it said with regard to someone whose faults and shortcomings are generally known, "and so little virtue!" Alas! the fact is that it is a matter of Communions received out of routine and of Communions badly prepared for, which do not resemble in anything that for which our Lord instituted them, namely, to be the union of two sacrifices in the unity of a common sacrifice, that of the Head and that of the member. The Eucharist does not miraculously infuse good habits ready-made, but it instead—and at the very same time that it gives us our Savior, which is not the point under discussion—gives us the aptitude to acquire, by virtue of grace, certain strong habits which will cost us dear to acquire. It has not been instituted by our Savior in order that we may evade effort, or in order that we may be delivered from the necessity of taking pains, but in order that we may become capable of effort and be able to exert ourselves more.

Holy Communion gives us grace. It is for us to make use of this grace. It is like capital; if we let it lie dormant instead of utilizing it, we do not obtain its maximum effect. We have been enriched by a source of power of the first order. It still remains for us to develop this source of power.

It is in this sense that we can and ought to say: the fundamental condition for deriving the maximum benefit from the Eucharist is the state of sacrifice, in other words, the previous or the concomitant placing of the soul in an atmosphere of generosity that permits the presence of the Master to produce its entire effect.

We can reason in the same way with respect to the sacrament of Penance. Can one maintain that it dispenses with the virtue of penance? Not at all. The matter of the sacrament is not any sort of confession but a contrite Confession. The more intense the contrition is and the higher its motive, the greater is the benefit of the accusation to the soul.

The sacrament of Penance does not act like water which removes once for all the stains from a garment without the danger of their return. Propensities to evil remain in the penitent. The effect of a good Confession is not only to wash away faults but to introduce into the soul the love of God and the hatred of what offends Him, at least in a sufficient measure and to the extent of a minimum, imperfect contrition.

It is precisely because we can never be certain of having a contrition sufficiently complete that the Church sanctions the accusation of the same sin several times. The problem, then, is to have recourse to the Sacrament of Penance not in order to dispense ourselves from repenting and amending our lives but rather to repent and to amend throughout our lives.

Facing Life

Let us conclude. The helps God gives us are indeed precious. It remains for us to avail ourselves of them with a proper spirit. All the verbs that concern our destiny are reflexive verbs: we work out *our own* salvation, we damn *ourselves*, we sanctify *ourselves*. Of ourselves and without grace we can do nothing. But we must, each one of us, render possible and fully effective the action of the divine aids.

"God created us without us," said St. Augustine, "but he did not will to save us without us." Our purpose has been to recall this and to emphasize, because certain persons too often forget it, our participation in the ascent in grace and in the efficacy of the supernatural means placed by God at our disposal to make of us virtuous souls and saints.

To know how to endure

At the time of the Calvinistic struggle in Vivarais, before the coming of Henry IV, King of France, the Jesuit Jacques Salès was arrested and massacred for his faith, particularly because of his preaching on the Eucharist. A good lay brother named Saultemouche, who served him for a companion, did not want to let him have the honor of martyrdom alone, and so he also claimed the privilege of being led to torture. The torments which both had to undergo were excruciating, and Saultemouche encouraged himself saying: "Endure! Endure!" He had the courage to endure till the end, and his name is found beside that of Père Jacques Salès in the martyrology. We cannot compare our sufferings with those of such brave heroes, but we can be inspired profitably by the courageous prayer of the generous brother. In the midst of our thousand difficulties and our little or great annoyances, we can say, "Endure! Endure!"

Endure! In the first place, through good sense and sound philosophy. What is the use of rebelling? In any event, we must accept what comes. Events dominate us; we are not the masters of them. To recriminate, to sigh, and to protest are ineffective actions. Like the Stoics, we must recognize that suffering passes, accomplishing its work, and it seems to laugh at our lamentations or refusals.

Endure! Through a supernatural spirit, because our crosses unite us to our Lord's Cross. God sends or permits suffering only to give us the opportunity to identify ourselves with His Son. Moreover, even humanly speaking, suffering well accepted makes us mature; it demands rare virtues. As long as a man has had nothing but happiness, he does not know of what he is capable, just as we do not really know what the sound of a bell is as long as the clapper has not struck it. But let sorrow come upon a man;

Facing Life

then he can divine what he is capable of doing. When the soul is fortified by divine motives, it can reach that summit which humanity can reach in the way of moral uplift. For the sons of men, as for the Son of Man, the highest royalty comes from the crown of thorns.

Endure! Through charity for all your brethren. While it permits us to "fill up those things that are wanting of the sufferings of Christ" (Col. 1:24), suffering gives us a most efficacious role in the Redemption. To act safely is virtuous; but to suffer, how much more! The great instrument of salvation is the acceptance of the cross on which one is to be nailed. If we had more often present in our mind the sufferings of all our brethren scattered throughout the world, how much more cheerful would we be in accepting the many miseries which assail us!

Franz Liszt, the incomparable musician, received minor orders after leading a very disorderly life. He resonates not only to the accents of the interior harmonies that well up within him but to all the suffering appeals that rise from the universe. He writes, "I preserve, active and very deep-rooted, the sense of compassion which makes me resonate intensely to human suffering. Sometimes, for short moments, I experience those [sufferings] of the sick in the hospital, of the wounded in war, and even of those condemned to torture or to death. It is something analogous to the stigmata of St. Francis—minus the ecstasy that belongs only to the saints."

It is necessary to have endured evil, in general at least, in order to sympathize with the suffering of others, especially with the sufferings which one does not immediately witness. Personal suffering, if one has the courage to persevere through it, furnishes antennae and puts one in sympathy with the sorrows of others. This is a magnificent privilege belonging to those who suffer.

Whatever may happen, let us learn how to endure. Let us say like the good brother: "Endure, my poor body! Endure, my poor soul, until your entrance into Beatitude. Only the brave will carry off the victory. Endure!"

In very trying moments, look upon the Master's Cross.

During the course of the First World War, the following event took place one day. An ambulance stopped at the side of a road. From a cross, which had been struck by a shell some days before, there hung, just about to fall, an old wooden image of Christ. His emaciated body, marked by the scars of time, was no longer held by the nails of the hands. The body leaned to one side and bore the distressed aspect of one who asked for help.

The driver had finished changing his wheel and was wiping his hands, which were plastered with sticky mud. He looked curiously at the sunken cheeks and the deep-set eyes, to which the sculptor of the august face wanted to transfer long ago a suffering expressive of extreme martyrdom. Suddenly, he perceived that someone had twined some barbed wire on the head of Christ, as if to give Him a crown of fresh thorns, and he could not refrain from smiling.

Then, thinking of all the misery in the world:

"And Thou," he murmured, "what dost Thou think of it?"

A long minute passed.

"Let's go! Quick! To work!" And he bent down to turn the crank.

Christ is leaning over all our paths. From His lookout of mercy, He watches us poor human beings as we grope along the path of trial which we all must walk. This path He willed to travel first, while the heavy wood of the Cross dug into His shoulder.

What consolation to know that there is One who appreciates our suffering, takes note of each effort, and helps us to bear the pains! Will we ever know how many times the sight of the crucifix has raised the courage of someone?

Unfortunately, the story of the driver has a sequel. Scarcely had he returned to his wheel when the driver saw a straggler who perceived the crucified Christ and began to kick lightly at the support of the cross, already so tottering. Then, as he went away, with a wicked look in his eye, the man pulled at the leg. Scarcely had the straggler taken three steps when, with a dull thump of wood that breaks, the crucifix fell, and the face of the Crucified landed in the mud of the road.

No one has ever told whether the columns of soldiers which went up the road later on were more gallant, because from the roadside had disappeared the two protecting arms and the tearful face of the Savior on the Cross, the friend of all who carry their crosses.

In company with the Cyrenean

What a comfort it is to look at Christ when one is suffering. But there is even something better to do, and that is to share with Christ and to offer ourselves to Him in order to share His suffering. It is no longer a question of using His Cross to console us but to avail ourselves of our crosses to comfort Him. It is the game reversed, it is the knowledge that the Redemption is a work of many and that to the sacrifice of the Head, the members of Christ are called to join their sacrifices.

A novelist once imagined the following story. Christ decided to die for man and He is in the act of

Facing Life

accomplishing His sacrifice. They have lifted Him up onto the gibbet, and from that bloody height, He sees the wickedness of the world. The centuries are being unfolded, and no one, or hardly anyone, will understand the price of the Blood that is shed by the Lamb of God. Sensual vices continue to be, and the sins of pride and hatred rise to combat in meaningless and endless strife, and one would say almost "for the pleasure of it." He who thirsts for purity, humility, and charity is suddenly seized by a terrible anger. There is nothing to look upon but the soldiers who play at dice, the Herods who feast, the Pilates who fear for their own skin, the Peter who has denied Him, the apostles who have fled, the Judas who hangs himself. There is nothing to hear but the exchange of thoughts regarding Him. He discovers that the inhabitants of the sinister planet, the earth, are not worth the trouble of being saved. He withdraws His feet from the nails which hold them, disengages His hands, leaps to the earth, and takes hold of His tunic so violently that the dice roll far away on the slope of the hill. He ascends into Heaven. The Cross remains empty. In the last hour, wearied by the stupidity and baseness of humanity, the Redeemer gives up on the Redemption. The world does not merit to possess a Savior dying for it.

Uncommon Virtue

Ah! How far we are from the reality of the story. The people? Jesus excuses them. The executioners? "Father, forgive them, for they know not what they do!" (Luke 23:34). The apostle Peter and his triple denial? Jesus is ready to ask him three times if He can count on his love. Judas? The Savior called him his friend, and He is completely ready to pardon Him, as He does Peter, at the least sign of repentance.

No, no, Jesus is not going to unfasten Himself! He has declared that He will go even to the end, *in finem*, even to the consummation of His work. He will not leave the Cross before the *Consummatum est*. If Mary, who was so much distressed to see Him hung upon the Cross, a prey to the dreadful gangrene on the gibbet of infamy, had attempted to unfasten Him, our Savior would have reascended the frightful throne of His glory in order to redeem us.

In vain, the world maligns, censures, and does not understand. It has need of His Blood even to the last drop. The divine Master will not be sparing of it.

But what anguish to think of the lack of fruit—relative, of course, but apparently so cruel—of the Redemption; fruit which the Savior had wanted to be so copious! A Redeemer whose work is of infinite value, and yet a Redemption which is not being brought about and which spends its time in not being realized! A formidable mystery, concerning which St. Paul wrote: "[I] fill up those things that are wanting of the sufferings of Christ, in my flesh" (Col. 1:24). It is very clear that the apostle does not speak of himself alone. To complete the Passion of Christ is a task incumbent on all of us. Our Lord, who obviously was able to save the world without our participation, has deigned to will that we come to His assistance. If He wished to unite all of us to His person in the unity of a single Mystical Body — "I am the vine: you the branches" (John 15:5) — it is because He intended to unite us all to His work, the work of salvation.

We are not only the redeemed but also redeemers. Because we are members of Christ, every one among us has the mission of cooperating with Christ, the divine Head, in the Redemption of all mankind.

It is a magnificent mission and it constitutes our most beautiful title. It is a most important mission. If we do not play our part as we should, if we do not participate with all the force expected from our effort, if we do not agree to "fill up" that which is lacking, a sad lack will be the result. There will be a vacant place in the Redemption. Certain souls will not be saved as God has wished; certain other souls will not be sanctified as much as the Lord has wished. Every one of us is a master of the world.

Uncommon Virtue

Do we know it? Do we bear it in mind? How do we live so as to serve as a genuine "fulfillment of the Savior?" To have been consecrated on the day of our Baptism as an authentic prolongation of Christ is not a trifle! Since Christ is the Redeemer, the only Savior, to say that we make only one with that only One, that we have been "Christianized" by that Head: is not this equivalent of saying that we have been at the same time "Redeemerized" or "Saviorized," if one will pardon these awkward words?

Most assuredly, the participation of the Head, our Lord, and of us, the members, is not of the same nature. The merits of our Lord are of strict justice, ours of mere fitness, but because the Savior has deigned to ask for our merits, these complementary merits have become necessary. If they are in default, the Redemption is just that much hindered or slowed.

Ah! How necessary it would be for some Cyreneans to aid the Savior of the world! Who wishes to volunteer for this work? These Cyreneans are the men whom the world needs: they are those whose name is written at the top of the page in the Book of Life. The blind world does not even suspect it.

Among the countless stories that are found on the margins of the Gospel is the following. When Simon of Cyrene met the procession which led Jesus to His crucifixion, he was on his way to a meeting in which the future guardian of the gateway to the Temple was to be chosen. As he was not present at the meeting, it happened that another man was chosen. When Simon returned home, his wife heaped insults upon him and asked, "Why did you have to carry the Cross of that young Galilean carpenter?" He answered, "I was called upon to do so by the centurion." To this his wife said, "Perhaps so! But after that, why did you delay?" Simon said, "Because of some strange words which that young man uttered. Weighed down by affliction, He did not pity Himself, and His words made me forget all the rest." His wife said, "You are very foolish! Here is what you have probably gained by it! Your father and your father's father have been guardians of the gateway to the Temple, and their names will be preserved forever in the registers. But you alone of your line of descendants will be forgotten. After your death, no one will hear the name of Simon of Cyrenean!"

The history that men write takes little note of the redeeming power of the saints and of the primary role of those who support Christ as He ascends the Cross. But God is a better judge, and it is His judgment that is important. Sometimes, even here below, He permits that those

Uncommon Virtue

who have "filled up" the Passion in a more resplendent or more efficacious manner may become known. Their haloes eclipse the most beautiful diadems. But what does it matter whether the world ever speaks of us, provided our pilgrimage here below is that of a soul thirsting for redemption? What does it matter whether our help be without a name, provided only that it be efficacious!

VI

Magnanimity in Suffering

To face life courageously is difficult even for the man who is in possession of all his forces and who enjoys good health. Do we realize what heroism is demanded of those whom illness strikes down and constrains to long months in the hospital or to the solitude of an isolation room?

Grappling with ill-health

When on an educational trip or on an excursion in the French or Swiss Alps, did you ever visit one of those plateaus on which modern medicine has placed those institutions that are half-hotel and half-hospital, called sanatoriums?

Up there on the mountain, there are some people who are interested only in the peaks, the rocky pinnacles, the glaciers, the altitude, and all that nature has to offer. There is enough to charm those who are the hardest to please, enough to swell the enthusiasm of the lovers of mountain peaks! Yet in these mountains, there are other summits than those of basalt, limestone, or granite. In the midst of the necessarily mixed and sometimes strange population of the sanatoriums, it is difficult to know of what moral elevation certain consumptives, men and women to whom God has sent the terrible cross of tuberculosis, so terrible and so gloriously transforming, are capable.

One who has not actually seen the order and life of a sanatorium can form an idea of it by reading Thomas Mann's *The Magic Mountain*.[44] No part is better analyzed or expressed more surely than the sensation of indefinite duration, which is the great cross.

The inmate of a sanatorium, especially if he is bedridden, is, as it were, placed outside of time. In the novel, Joachim Ziemssen, a beloved friend, thanks Hans Castrop for his visit:

"This is an event for me. I mean a break, a mark in this eternal and infinite anthem...."

"But time must pass rather quickly for you," says Hans Castrop.

[44] Cf. Thomas Mann, *The Magic Mountain*, translated from the German by H. T. Lowe-Porter (New York: Alfred A. Knopf, 1947).

Magnanimity in Suffering

"Quickly or slowly, as you like," replied Joachim, "I mean that it does not pass at all. There is no time here, and there is no life."

Elsewhere, Joachim says that "the smallest unit of time is the month." They cannot think of a sick person coming for only a few days. If that were the case, it would only be one of the ordinary people of the town, someone "from below" who has nothing to do with the realm of the "people up above."

Later, concerning the unfailing regularity of life in the sanatorium, the author expresses the philosophy of monotony. He explains how long stretches of time, when their course is an unbroken monotony, shrivel up in a measure which mortally frightens a man. When one day is like all, they are only a single day. In a perfect uniformity, the longest life would seem very short and would pass in the twinkling of an eye. The introduction of changed habits or of new habits is the only means at the patients' disposal to refresh their perception of time.

These thoughts are applied to the life of the sick person. When a man spends a long time in bed as a patient, the long series of days passes very quickly. It is the same day that is repeated incessantly. But as it is always the same day, it is not very correct to speak of a repetition. It is better to speak of infinity, of an immovable present, of eternity. The nurses bring in soup for breakfast, just as they brought it in yesterday and just as they will bring it in tomorrow. At the same moment, the patient is seized by a sort of dizziness. While he sees the breakfast coming, the forms of time are lost, and that which is unveiled as the true form of existence is a fixed present in which someone will bring in the soup eternally.

The patient is as if possessed by the haunting memory of this duration. It flows in such an extraordinarily uniform manner that he cannot see it pass. In the novel, at the approach of Christmas, someone says that there are six weeks before the stars of Christmas night will shine. It is said in answer that they speak of six weeks, of not even as many weeks as there are days in a week. What is one of those weeks, one of those little cycles from Monday to Sunday and again to Monday? What is a day, counted from the moment when one sits down at the breakfast table to the return of that moment twenty-four hours later? Nothing, although they were twenty-four hours. What is an hour spent in taking a rest, a walk, or a meal? Again, it is nothing! The total of these nothings cannot be taken seriously.

The author adds that this is serious only when we go down the scale to the smallest degree. The seven times sixty seconds during which the patient holds the thermometer between his lips for the record on the temperature chart make life hard and burdensome. They expand so as to form a small eternity.

Magnanimity in Suffering

They insert periods of solidity in the quick flight and the shadowy game of time. Ah! Those minutes during which it is necessary, each day, to keep the thermometer under the tongue in order to measure the degree of fever. By some diabolical irony, they become interminable, when the remainder of the day stretches out as if it were beyond duration!

The patient looks at his wrist watch. It is nine thirty-six. He waits for those seven minutes to pass by. He walks up and down in his room with the thermometer under his tongue. It seems as if time drags along; the delay seems infinite. Two minutes and a half have passed, and he looks at the hands of his watch, fearing lest he has let the moment pass. He does a thousand things, takes up some objects and replaces them. He goes out on the balcony; he looks at the mountains with their peaks, the line of crests and rocky surfaces. He looks toward the roads and the flower beds on the terrace, the rocky grotto; he listens to a murmur which came up from the solarium and then goes back again to his room.

Let us make a long story short.

With a great deal of pain and effort, the sick man seems to help the minutes along, to push them, and make them advance. Six minutes have finally passed. But as he is lost, in a reverie, standing in the middle of his room, and lets his thoughts wander, the last-minute escapes, unperceived, with the quickness of a cat.

In this picture of monotony, it is necessary to place other sufferings and crosses: treatments, pneumothorax, phrenicotomy, thoracoplasty, hypodermic injections, absence from home, and companions who may not always be agreeable. In the midst of such a purgatory, there are souls of extraordinary spirituality, souls that sing and attain the highest peaks of moral grandeur.

Some examples

We glean from a voluminous correspondence certain notes and letters among many others. We shall betray no secrets, and perhaps we shall be helpful in encouraging some dejected souls.

A young priest on the foreign missions has labored for eight years under the burning sun of the Indies. His superiors have taken him away from his Christians that he might come to France to recuperate, but he suffers from not being any longer able to preach the faith in the Far East which drained his strength. But he knows that Christ saved more souls on the Cross than on His long walks through the towns of Galilee. The most fruitful apostolate is not that of the word, but that of suffering. His silence in bed or on his reclining chair converts more pariahs and Brahmins than

Magnanimity in Suffering

his most laborious catechetical instructions in Tamil. He wastes away cheerfully, a Francis Xavier of a new type, on the feverish shore of the Sancian[45] where God nails him.

In another sanatorium, four boys have a common room. Two of them are seminarians; a third has a brother who is a priest; the fourth is a Boy Scout. We speculate whether lying in an invalid's bed answers their need to rush forth and hasten to the vineyard of the Lord! The Master wants them there: His ways are not our ways. They will do in their state as much as is desired!

Elsewhere, there is a young Jesuit. He has undergone an operation on his lung which has been only partly successful, and he sees himself immobilized for many days perhaps. His father died, but he could not assist him in his dying moment. His brother is going to be ordained a priest, but he must give up being present at this celebration which he so eagerly looked forward to. He frets and would like to escape! Blessed are all these sacrifices, for souls, far or near, must gather fruit from them.

Another patient has already undergone one thoracoplasty and must submit to it again. He can do little but think of

---

[45] Sancian, modern Shangchuan, is the Chinese island on which St. Francis Xavier died.

Uncommon Virtue

it, and his soul says in agony: "Take, Lord Jesus, and receive ... *Sume, Domine, et suscipe.*" That is a royal road. Is it not necessary to accept everything with joy for the divine King?

Men, young men, priests, seminarians, religious—from these, one may expect an extraordinary courage. But here are women and girls whose bravery is equal if not superior. A young girl, twenty years of age, has taken care of herself since the age of fifteen. Soon she will have to submit to a thoracoplasty. She is admirable in faith and in resignation. She never speaks of her condition but quietly performs a thousand services for her companions. Another has already submitted twice to a thoracoplasty and must submit to a third one. She possesses an extraordinary energy and declares herself ready to undergo it. Being a burden to two sisters and having no personal resources, she wishes to use the most extreme means in order to get cured quickly and to help her sisters.

Another young girl, brimming over with life, activity, and intelligence, has been confined to bed for long months and has just had a pulmonary relapse accompanied by a white swelling on the knee. She maintains a courage and a cheerfulness that nothing can stop. She is a member of the U.C.M.[46] and gives

[46] *Union Catholique des Malades*, an association of sick people, grouped in tens, who correspond with each other for mutual diversion, support, and encouragement.

Magnanimity in Suffering

courses by correspondence to the downhearted of Berck.[47] To one of her friends who interrogates her, she replies that she desires neither to live nor to die, that she lets the good Lord choose, and that it is a great grace for her to be ill, because, with her nature, she would have perhaps been lost in the world.

How many others there are whose angelic patience we can see. They seldom express the reasons for such lofty virtue but humbly guard for God alone the modesty of their secret garden! First, a brief note from one patient: "I have seen the doctor these days; there is much to be desired in my condition. They are going to take me back to the hospital where I shall not move about so much. I shall not be able to leave in September, and they will perhaps order me to take treatments for tuberculosis. Pray for me, because this news pains me. I offer all for souls, but it is hard. I think especially of the sorrow that this news will cause my mother and my dear ones." This fine ending gives full expression to his feeling: "I shall bear up against everything."

Here is how another patient speaks: "After having lost my beloved mother, two brothers, and a sister, I have only my father left, and he has been ill and bedridden for thirteen months. But God, in His infinite goodness, while

---

[47] A commune in northern France.

sending me this trial, has given me each day the strongest will and joy to love Him more and to want to love Him more and more. Therefore, complete abandonment to His will becomes so much easier. I desire nothing and, if God does not wish to cure me, I ask Him to give me the strongest courage to suffer better."

Finally this last document: "My father, your letter has helped me to take one more step toward the *Magnificat*. I have said to our Lord that I was happy under this heavy cross, since it could increase His glory a little. This has not been without difficulty. The effort was great, very great. I could not refrain from lamenting while I was crushed by this immense suffering.... In my moments of solitude, I say to Jesus a weak 'Thank you' for uniting me so closely to His Passion. A kind of peacefulness comes over me then, because I think that a little more of me has become Jesus Christ. What you here told me about the Host, whose substance must be changed in order that it may be Jesus Christ alone, has done me some good. A perfect host is what I should want to be."

If anyone can find more beautiful sentiments, let him tell us of them. How fortunate it is for us that in our poor world there is infinitely more of the sublime than the novelists can discover and the mass of people imagine.

Magnanimity in Suffering

Two names among many

Among all the unnamed persons, there is sometimes one figure or the other that emerges. By God's permission, the public is led to know something of their valor.

Here are two great patients. The word "great" qualifies less the infirmity of their bodies than the magnitude of their souls: One is a boy laid low at the age of twenty-four; the other is a man struck down by death at fifty-five. Both are face to face with suffering and are animated by a superhuman courage. They are named Henri d'Hellencourt and André Bach. Fragments of their intimate notes permit us to follow their spiritual itinerary.[48]

Let us recall for an instant these two captivating figures.

Henri d'Hellencourt

French Scout at the Collège Stanislas[49] in Paris since his eleventh birthday, Henri d'Hellencourt became successively chief of a patrol, road scout, leader of the "20th," leader of the senior troop, and finally, in 1935, assistant scoutmaster of his group. All this tells us a great deal about the quality of his character.

---

[48] Henri d'Hellencourt, *Journal de bord*. André Bach, *Le royaume de Dieu est parmi vous* (texts presented by M. Nedoncelle). Both volumes published by Bloud et Gay: Paris, 1941.

[49] An elite private primary and secondary school.

Uncommon Virtue

Unhappily, a secret illness consumed him by slow degrees. The boy who was so desirous of expansion and of the exterior apostolate was forced to reduce his activity little by little. He had to spend long months in the country. Even when he lived in Paris, he often had to limit his scout work to receiving his comrades. Not being able to share their life in the open, he had to content himself with listening to accounts of their hikes and camps. Henri's whole career was spent between his fifteenth and his twenty-fifth years. Providence needed this time to lead this fiery youth to that plenitude of abandonment which is the plenitude of virtue.

We remember the words of St. Teresa of the Child Jesus: "They had told me that I would not have any agony. I wish very much to have it." "If you should have to choose?" "I would choose nothing."

These are sincere words, but they are rare. They were, however, those of Henri d'Hellencourt. Three months before his death, he writes, "To accept is not to submit; it is to construct. That word contains for me no grief and no regret. For me, it has the sound of a victory, of a conquest." He was a brave young man who found such expressions and reached such a loving and complete resignation! He was, in truth, a victorious soul.

The battle was not won at the very beginning but from the beginning, and we can see his riches.

Magnanimity in Suffering

He realized that his Christianity was more traditional and routine-like than doctrinal and personal. He decided to study his religion. He came to "feel" it, but he did not "know" it sufficiently. A friend procured for him *Christ, the Life of the Soul* by Dom Marmion; and he understood that in it is the strong doctrine which is the substance of Christian living. He writes: "If I could, I would read the whole book this evening, so eager am I to know."

He reached the age of twenty. On November 20, 1936, he notes again: "*Christ, the Life of the Soul* fires me with enthusiasm. The great mystery and the great reality of Christ touch me very much. I devour the pages with delight."

To know the gift of God is much, but a man must live by it. And our road-scout applied himself to it:

A new week begins; it is necessary for me to advance spiritually. Three points:

> The good God: fervent prayer in the morning, when I cannot communicate; a quarter of an hour rest after breakfast to regain strength, to put myself in the presence of God; to realize at each instant His abiding presence.
>
> Not to think any more about B — is impossible. I have even a duty to think about her, to pray for her.

> But no idle dreams ... no unrealizable projects for the moment. To place everything that regards her first of all on the spiritual plane.
>
> Work: to tie myself down each day to the work undertaken, beginning by that which bores me, doing it well ... persistency in activity.

You will note the paragraph in which he mentions the young girl whom he had dreamed of making the mother of his children. He suspects that God has other designs and checks his quickly beating heart. That youth was a wise man.

Scouting guided and dominated him in everything! Often he breathed this prayer: "Lord, make me be a good leader.... Jesus, give me the grace to think of others before thinking of myself.... The state of my health is a great obstacle to my work. Let me take care of it while avoiding all idleness."

From time to time, when his illness obliged him to use more precautions, nature rebelled a little: "All that I endure I regard much more as a withdrawal than as a gift." And again: "This disease consumes me. It kills me instead of making me be reborn." He is accusing himself and wishes to correct himself: "I shall fight to the last drop of energy."

The thought of the young girl who for an instant enchanted his dreams of the future comes back to him:

Magnanimity in Suffering

"To live without earthly love. If that is what God asks of me, He will send me the necessary strength for that to be possible. I am learning my occupation in life at this moment."

He began with the study of law in order to prepare himself, to the best of his ability, for a future career: "I must work," he notes, "even when it will tire me."

In spite of the solitude that should have hastened his union with God, he did not find himself sufficiently recollected. "I should profit by my way of life in order to discipline my character, to keep silence often, and to listen to the interior voice of the Holy Spirit counseling me." Always practical, as was his custom, he writes: "I am going to begin again to read the Gospel. When I have some free moments, I open it at random and read, even if it be only ten lines."

La Spiritualité de la Route, the stirring work by Joseph Folliet, stimulated him, and he wished to practice the asceticism taught by it in his room. "Physical effort forbids this, as does intellectual effort to a certain degree, but moral effort does not." Sometime later, he has the joy of noting, "My will has been quickened, my resolution has become firm. I ask God to give me the necessary strength to go on with this work of molding myself which I have undertaken and which has no other aim but to glorify Him."

Uncommon Virtue

On December 8, 1936, he writes: "I feel the need of making a real retreat, to recall to mind the great doctrine of sanctifying grace." In January, 1937, he enjoyed being able to spend a few days of recollection at the abbey of Solesmes.

"I seek Thee, O my God." He remembered the counsel that someone gave him to adapt his illness to his religion and his religion to his illness. A young priest who had formerly been a scoutmaster told him about his own vocation, and this lit up still better that of the young retreatant. There is a ministry of suffering; our Lord asks us to complete His Passion: "My God, I want to walk the way Thou hast traced for me, but I have not the courage."

The idea of the gift, the complete gift, became more and more pressing: "My God, I have feared Thee and my destiny. I have dreamed of a great life. My mistake was to want it to be great for myself. It will be great if I give it, if I give it to Thee, so that Thou canst make of it what it ought to be."

His resolution was "To rise up higher. For that, I must enter the desert." Henri writes to his father on Sunday, January 17, 1937: "After the close of my retreat, I decided to play for two years the 'game of the desert'.... Since circumstances force me to remain in bed, I shall make up for my losses by playing a great interior adventure." His sick room would be his desert "above measure," and he counted off, first, the

Magnanimity in Suffering

imposed physical suffering, then the solitude, the use of sufferings for the communion of saints, the abandonment of the affections, the renunciation of comforts, the works, and the service "to the caravan"—dressing the wounds of some and raising the spirits of others.

We cannot tell in detail what that touching game was; we must read his *Journal de bord*, and especially the pages in which he describes the adventure. Having before him an image of Fr. de Foucauld, he notes: "His look penetrates me and confides to me the great secret." By silence and generous efforts, each day he advanced in love.

To give is not yet sufficient, and Henri understood that. We must give cheerfully, and he planned to write *A Game of Joy* in order to encourage others to live.

"I feel myself more and more attracted to spiritual things.... I have added to the notion of the desert another notion, that of recollection." God indicated more and more His hold on this generous youth, but something in him still resisted: "I am so afraid of abandoning self in order to give myself entirely to Thee." This was the resistance that arose from feeling and not from the will. "Thanks, my God, for this increase in illness and suffering which Thou art sending me.... If God calls on me to divest myself, it is to clothe me again with Himself." Therefore, it must not be halfheartedly. It was at the price of his gift of self without reserve that he experienced a holy joy: "Thou hast given me joy. Never have I been so happy as in these hours of suffering when Thou hast leaned over me; Thou hast drawn me into Thy ways."

After some improvement, Henri returned from Perche to Paris, but more frequent crises told him that perhaps without delay the joys of earth would be followed by the joys of Heaven. He would struggle still for some months. He writes, "Inflame me with Thy love, I implore. Inflame me till I die from it!" On the morning of January 11, 1940, the angel of death called him. Shortly before his death, he said to his father, "It is necessary to despoil oneself," and his father replied, "You have always accepted trials with generosity." Henri answered: "That is true, I have never said 'No.'"

André Bach

André Bach was another who never said "No." Like Henri d'Hellencourt, but with a more energetic step and a greater maturity because of the powerful help of the priesthood — he would rise by suffering to the heights of love.

His father was from Aveyron, and André was born in Seine-et-Oise on July 30, 1884. He first studied for the medical profession, but during his preparation for the preliminary medical examination, Huysmans' *Pages catholiques* came into his hands. There he discovered the beauty of the Church. It is in a poetic way that he narrates the event thus: "Suddenly, before any strange feminine vision ever made my heart beat, the *reality of the Church*"—it is he who emphasizes the words—"for the first time appeared to me, like a white cloistered nun, very pure and redeeming."

He continues: "Until then, my young heart could be placed anywhere; from that hour, it was fixed. For me, from that instant, there will never be any sovereign mistress of my thoughts but the divinely instituted Church." Thinking of the young women whom he met among the students or who went with his comrades, he declares: "It is not they who will ever separate me, even for a second, from this sole devotion."

Henri d'Hellencourt had to detach himself: that was a more difficult thing. André neither had the time nor the inclination to fall in love with anyone. At the age of love, the Church conquered his love, and the gift was never regretted or taken back.

In October, he entered the major seminary of Issy. His Excellency, Msgr. Feltin, Archbishop of Bordeaux, in the preface to his book, expressed his pride in having been the classmate of André Bach.

Uncommon Virtue

Would André be a priest of the secular clergy or a religious? He thought for a moment about the Benedictines, but he believed he would do better by being a parish priest. On December 1, 1915, when he was held a prisoner in Chemnitz,[50] he told this to his mother: "I shall not seek in an atmosphere of self-preservation an external aid for my weakness. In fact, I believe that it is harder and more difficult to be what I aspire to be, simply a 'Catholic priest,' rather than to be a religious of any order whatsoever, and my mind is made up."

We need not find fault with his expression "Catholic priest;" the religious belongs to the priesthood as much as does the secular priest. We understand what he meant. It is in the ministry of the parish priest that the Abbé André Bach believed himself called to sanctify himself. It is no secret that in the life he embraced, he did not always find the constant realization of the ideal he dreamed of. It is a price paid by the finest institutions that they not be served by all with the enthusiasm and intensity that they deserve. A man quickly limits his horizon and contents himself with mediocrity. André, at least, did not fail to go to the limit of the demands made by his priestly vocation.

---

[50] Chemnitz, Germany is home to a German prisoner-of-war camp that was used during the First World War.

Magnanimity in Suffering

The ordinary baptized person is a unique splendor: "By our incorporation through baptism we have become Christs. We are Christs in the midst of our brethren." For the laity called to remain in the world but resolved to live there in the fullness of Jesus Christ, André instituted a sort of association and gave the five following points as a rule:

1. Regard your daily work as the lay sisters and lay brothers do in the monasteries: to furnish help to the Church.
2. Offer your sufferings in atonement for the sins of each day.
3. Strive for an hour in the morning and an hour in the afternoon to see our Lord in your neighbor.
4. Avail yourself of your study club (which he desired to meet weekly) in order to know Christ better in His own person as Head and in that of His members.
5. At every Mass, dedicate yourself to a watchful observance of the above points."

Even before he was visited by suffering, the Abbé Bach seemed to have received the grace to understand its importance in the spiritual life:

Uncommon Virtue

When men are faced with suffering, what are we to tell them?

If they are unbelievers, we know of only one thing to tell them: the attitude of de Vigny's *Wolf*.... Suffering is the inescapable lair for all men. It is of no avail to lament or to complain. We must act in a manner that befits the dignity of our human nature.

For those who believe: reveal to them the mystery of the Redemption; point out to them the Passion of our Lord, which continues in them, [and] Christ who is in them, with them.... Make them see the compensating and redeeming power of their suffering, not only for their own sins but for all the sins of others."

For the use of the sick, the Abbé drew up an answer to an imaginary but practical questionnaire. Here are a few of its questions:

SUFFERER: Is it not very important for me to remain conscious of my role in the Church?

ANSWER: Very important. Moreover, you will have no real consolation except on that condition. My dear sick people, we have to continue the physical suffering endured by the Savior during His Passion.

Magnanimity in Suffering

SUFFERER: Does the world need those who suffer?

ANSWER: It needs them urgently, as does also our Lord. He is fully aware of their state of suffering, and without them, He would no longer be able to continue to live wholly in the world."

To have high ideas about sick people and about their role of suffering in general in the world is not very difficult; but to conduct oneself rightly when illness and suffering actually visit him, that is the touchstone of true generosity.

In 1932, from St. Joseph's Hospital, to which a terrible disease of the trachea forced him to retire—and for how long?—he wrote:

> Never in my life, did I need so much interior strength just to live day by day, and at certain times hour by hour.... Shaken by painful fits of fever, brutally torn away from all my work, no longer able to celebrate Holy Mass, awaiting I do not know what painful treatment, no longer having any outlook for the future, my soul at certain hours pierced with intense sorrow, sometimes shedding tears.

How was he going to stand this complete dejection?

Uncommon Virtue

He faced it, but it was hard. God had pity on him. To the amazement of the doctors, a radium treatment cured him, or at least improved his condition to such an extent that he was able to resume his priestly work for five years more. He had been named vicar at St. Francis de Sales with the Abbé Loutel, who was also known under the pen name of Pierre l'Ermite, as curate.

Up to the day when the disease again attacked his throat, he spent himself without measure. Evidence of this may be found in the miscellany, compiled from plans and extracts of his sermons, his conversations, and his study clubs, which Nedoncelle dedicated to his memory. In November 1938, the unfortunate priest returned to St. Joseph's Hospital. All efforts at a cure were useless. In December, it was hoped that a tracheotomy would prolong his life, although at the cost of the complete loss of his voice. Nothing could be done, and he not only lost his voice but soon his life as well. However, God granted him four more months in which to perfect his virtue. Abbé Bach did not seek to be comforted; rather it was he who encouraged his visitors and the doctors who strove all in vain to give him relief: "When I entered his room in the morning," relates the surgeon who performed the operation, "I was terrified at my helplessness as a doctor.

Magnanimity in Suffering

The unheard-of thing took place that it was I who was comforted on leaving him."

The Abbé Loutil, his curate, relates as he knows how to do so well one of his conversations with the Abbé Bach when he visited him at St. Joseph's Hospital: "I am sad even to the tips of my hair," the Abbé had confided to him, and then added: "I did not imagine, that in the school of sorrow, there might be such a terrible class."

In order to talk about something, they exchanged a few words on the misfortunes of the times. The Abbé Loutil was alarmed about the quasi-impossibility to restore the Christian spirit to the masses. In some places, not only were they refusing to hear the Church, but they were even setting her shrines on fire. The vicar was not able to answer in words, so they gave him a slate. On it he wrote: "Before the churches in flames ... a new flame in the Church!"

"Must we not be alarmed about the lack of the virtue of charity on this wretched planet? Nations in a struggle against each other. The hatred that has accumulated through so many years!" the Abbé Loutil exclaimed. Again using the slate, he replied: "Humanity, in order not to founder, is faced with love. That day will be the rising tide coming from the depths of the deceptions of all hatreds."

Then, as if he had a prophetic vision, he wrote: "The Church will see a renewal, which will surpass that of the Middle Ages, because this time it will be universal."

And again these few lines: "My soul as a priest lives by that hope.... This, in short, is only my faith in the power of the love of Christ."

On his ordination picture, taken on July 3, 1909, the Abbé André Bach had written the words which Charles Péguy in *Le mystère de la charité de Jeanne d'Arc* puts on the lips of the maid struggling with the *Our Father*. Struck by the words *adveniat regnum tuum*, she says, "Father, how far off is the coming of Thy Kingdom!"

That was the cry of a young laborer who knew his strength for work in the vineyard of the Lord. On his small sickbed, the tone had changed: hope had become a certitude. The kingdom of God will come. But over and above the efforts of those who struggle is needed the more meritorious offering of those who are no longer able to struggle but accept their apparent uselessness. The Abbé had often helped his sick to enter into the great Pauline idea, the great Catholic idea: The chief aim of suffering is to help us to perfect the Passion of Christ. When this Passion has been completely perfected, that is, when the members of Christ, destined among many

Magnanimity in Suffering

for this redoubtable ministry of completing the Redemption, have played the game properly—to use an expression dear to Henri d'Hellencourt—then we can speak of an approaching advent of love upon the heart.

For his part, the Abbé André Bach desired nothing so much as to give to God all the redemptive suffering demanded by the needs of the hour. His suffering finally ended on May 14, 1937. The Abbé endured it without losing courage up to the end. He loved the phrase that one finds many times in his notes: "The priest who thirsts to be immolated." His immolation was complete.

We need to look about us not at those who suffer less but at those who suffer more, so as to be encouraged by their example.

In these times, when trouble knocks at every door, when because of privation physical pain abounds, and when an extreme dejection is besetting even the most valiant, it is a comfort for us to encourage one another by such beautiful examples of valor as André Bach and Henri d'Hellencourt.

In the midst of ills which had reached a terrible state of acuteness, Nietzsche put down these words: "It seems that nothing succeeds anymore to relieve me. The pains are by far too distracting! I say in vain: Endure all! I end by being disgusted with suffering itself. What we need is patience to sustain patience."

Thanks to their faith, our two great sufferers had the patience to sustain patience. We may say that the spirit of sacrifice was lacking in the generation between the two wars. In a period when heedless frivolity had the force of law, some still have shown that the seed of heroes and of saints is not lost.

VII

Love of Reparation

It is beyond doubt that a marked movement carries away a part of Catholic piety toward reparation. At this word, and facing this fact, some become enthusiastic. It is an opportunity for innumerable acts of generosity, but sometimes also, among some, for indiscreet acts of fervor. As usual, others remain inactive and indifferent. This is not for them. They want to live as Christians, but without all these *things on the side* of an excited and passing spirituality. Finally, there are some who are struck especially by the exaggerated practices of certain persons, or by the kind of language used by others, and become suspicious or make reservations.[51]

[51] We have purposely omitted in this work the words *host*, *victim*, and others of the same nature which many do not like in order to show that the doctrine of reparation is

We wish to recall to the mind of the last group that to make reparation is not in itself a question of sentiment but of dogma.

To the second group, we point out that to make reparation is not something optional or superfluous but rather a strict duty.

To the first group, we say that to make reparation is not an unhealthy or showy exaltation but clear-sighted and prudent generosity.[52]

The problem

To understand reparation well—we speak here of the theology of reparation—it is sufficient to understand well a brief phrase of St. Paul which is too often passed over for consideration through cowardice by some and through indifference or ignorance by the majority.

---

of itself independent of that vocabulary which can be used only with a proper understanding of it.

[52] For a more profound study, the reader is referred to the *Idée Reparatrice* (Beauchesne) and to *Le Sacré-Coeur et la Raparation* (Apostolat de la Prière). A magnificent example, but on the mystic plane, of a soul making reparation is found in *Consummata* (Marie-Antoinette de Geuser).

Love of Reparation

"[I] fill up those things that are wanting of the sufferings of Christ, in my flesh" (Col. 1:24; *adimpleo ea quae desunt passionum Christi*).

Supernatural life was lost for man. God is interested in restoring it to him. For this end, the Word, the second Person of the Blessed Trinity, will come on earth. By Original Sin, man has robbed the Most High of the glory which the super-naturalized creature owed to Him. Christ will make the compensation. He will be born in a manger, will live in poverty, will ascend a Cross, and His merits will repair the injury done to God by the disobedience of the first Adam. As a consequence, the sacrifice of the Savior will free mankind. It becomes capable again of living anew from divine life. The supernatural treasures are given back to it.

All that took place more than nineteen hundred years ago.

Let us here consider humanity for a moment. Each generation numbers a billion and a half people.[53]

I shall enumerate them.

Of this billion and a half, one billion does not know Jesus Christ; it is pagan or Mohammedan.

---

[53] The first edition of this book was originally published in 1950, at which time the world's population was estimated at roughly 2.5 billion.

Uncommon Virtue

There remain five hundred million, a half-million, the third of the entire number. Of this third, one-half is not Catholic but either schismatic or Protestant. There are left only about two hundred and sixty million people who practice the true religion of Jesus Christ. Again, of this number, that is, the number of the faithful, are they all truly faithful? The Savior has come to restore divine life to us. How many of those who call themselves faithful are in the state of grace?

If it is true that every individual of good faith who practices faithfully what he believes is the truth forms a part of the soul of the Church and *can* be saved, how many actually fulfill the conditions for salvation? Even in the Catholic Church, where the aids are more powerful than in false religions, how many lead an evil life and therefore render the Blood of Christ fruitless!

Yet the Savior has died for all. Nineteen hundred years ago, in His Agony, He offered Himself for the Redemption of the entire human race.

What a failure! From the height of His Cross, casting a glance into the future, the Savior could say to Himself, "I give all my Blood. And in almost two thousand years, this is what I have obtained: two-thirds of the world in ignorance. Half of the remaining third, in error; and my faithful so little faithful."

Love of Reparation

Alas, poor Jesus!

What! Were we in the presence of a real failure? Did the redeeming Blood not have its proclaimed power? To lower Himself to our nature by the Incarnation, did the all-powerful Word lose some of His power? Must we come to the conclusion that the Incarnation was a terrible failure?

Far from us be such sacrilegious blasphemy! The sacrifice of the Savior possesses an infinite value. The least step of the Son of God was sufficient, superabundantly sufficient, to redeem the world.

Yet the world is not redeemed! Every day, for nineteen hundred years, we have said, "Thy kingdom come, O my God!" What is more evident than this fact, that the Kingdom of God has not come? Without doubt the world is still young, and God is not in a hurry. But after all, for one who compares sacrifice and result, what a defeat! Such a tremendous effort for such a paltry result! Without a doubt again, in the order of charity, the mathematician need not be consulted. Who knows the value of a single act of love, the merit of one Holy Communion, the amount of glory procured for God by one life as a missionary or by one martyr's death?

Yet, these correctives do not satisfy. Another solution is necessary. Where is it?

Uncommon Virtue

"I fill up"

It is exactly here that the brief phrase of St. Paul, which we've already mentioned, is to be inserted: ""[I] fill up those things that are wanting of the sufferings of Christ, in my flesh" (Col. 1:24).

There is no failure on the part of our Lord. There is a failure on our part. It is not Christ who is at fault, it is ourselves. God could save the entire world without us. He has not wished it so.

To understand it well, let us lay aside for a moment the dogma of the Redemption in order to enter upon the dogma of the Mystical Body of Christ. Or rather, let us study the Redemption in the light of the Mystical Body.

It is to Christ that it belongs to save the world and to Him alone—but to *all* that is Christ.

Now, we Christians, by the very fact of our vocation as Christians, are part of Him.

Let us recall the vine and the branches, the members of the Body, and the substantial and closely related doctrine of our incorporation with Jesus Christ.

There is only one Savior, but I am a part of that Savior. Hence, in the Redemption of the world, I must contribute an effort of redemption.

Love of Reparation

Christ has come only for this: to save, to redeem, to reinstate—all these words are synonymous. But He has not been content to pay for us by our leaving *exteriors* to Him. He has united us to Himself, incorporated us with Himself. He has made us a part of Himself. One by one, He has grafted us upon Himself. On His Body nailed to the Cross, He has willed that bleeding notches might be made. It is thus that we are grafted on Him and that, by Him, the divine life which was once lost will penetrate us afresh and will make us live afresh in a divine manner.

Once redeemed, it is for us to become redeemers, to aid Christ whose members we became at the time of our redemption. It is by a close collaboration of all His members with Him that the Savior intends to realize His great work. He will perform the principal and the essential part; He will accumulate the merits. From us He will demand a participation, infinitesimal, yes, but which He wishes, through esteem for us, to render necessary. Thanks to that which we shall be very willing to give Him by our zeal, our prayers, and our sacrifices, this participation will consist in our bringing His infinite merits to souls.[54]

[54] Christ alone has merited for us *de condigno*, that is to say, in strict justice. Creatures, who can merit *de condigno*

Uncommon Virtue

There is a well-known comparison, but one that perhaps needs to be understood more thoroughly, meditated upon at length, and lived out in practice. It is that of the drop of water poured into the wine in the chalice. The wine represents the part of Christ in the Redemption of the world. The drop of water, our part. It is nothing, but it is required by law, and at the consecration it will be changed along with the wine into the Blood of Christ.

We see that every Christian *can* be a redeemer, a savior, a repairer with Christ. Every Christian *must* be a redeemer with Christ, a savior, a repairer.

To be a Christian and to persist in being uninterested in the Redemption of the world is a contradiction and a folly.

Alas! Because many Christians do not know this responsibility of their Christian vocation, or if they know it, they consider it as null and void, our Lord asks of some who are better informed or more generous to furnish Him a larger part of "those things that are wanting" for the Redemption of the world.

> *for themselves* the increase of sanctifying grace, can merit *for others* only *de congruo*. This problem has already been touched on at the end of chapter v.

Love of Reparation

In itself, nothing is lacking. In fact, our Lord deigns to have need of us to save our brethren. Because the majority of people flee from this obligation, the largest part of the work is required of a few. That is the reason for these extraordinary offers of our Lord to certain souls, a Margaret Mary, for example, or a Lidwina: "You, at least." As if the good Master said, "The others do not understand or do not want to. If you have understood, are you willing?"

We do not need to seek further for the secret of these magnificent vocations of souls or institutes dedicating themselves to reparation.

Here, we are far from a reparation that is performed out of pure sentiment or sheer fancy. They used to tell us: Exaltation, or even overdoing things. This is not the case. The truth is that it is a dogmatic matter and borders on a duty emanating directly from our role as Christians.

Pius XI and Margaret Mary

On May 8, 1928, Pope Pius XI issued an encyclical on reparation.[55] We can only refer to it here, but we will try to make the spirit of it understood.

---

[55] *Miserentissimus Redemptor*.

Uncommon Virtue

Let us present a scene that the convert Retté[56] gives of a mysterious person arriving in the early morning at a certain corner of the awakening countryside:[57]

It is a poor cluster of huddled houses, a village like any other village. The day dawned an hour ago. Unaccustomed to raise their thoughts on high and to pray, the workers are getting ready with heavy souls for a dull day. Those who have time are still walking about in their closed rooms, in spite of the rising sun. The parish priest has rung the bell in vain for Mass. Nobody, not even a choirboy appears. The sacrifice of the King of Heaven is going to be renewed with no one from this corner of the earth deigning even to think of it. Such is God, such is man. On hearing the bell, one of the freethinkers utters a blasphemy, while a hoarse cock begins to crow three times, doubtless to recall the treason committed that very night by one of the faithful.

Now there appears at the entrance to the village a figure in a long dark robe, a beggar's wallet at His side, His hair and beard unkempt, His bare feet leaving behind Him

[56] Adophe Retté (1863–1930), French poet and convert to Catholicism.
[57] *Sous l'étoile du matin*, preamble.

traces of Blood. The Man dressed in coarse cloth knocks at every door. Taking from His wallet a little white round wafer, He says to the one who comes to open the door: "I give you My Body and My Blood; give Me your heart in exchange." In many a place, the door is simply closed again without an answer. Here, an ugly kitchen maid spits in the face of the strange beggar; in another place, it is insults that He receives. The free-thinker throws a sharp bone at His head and wounds Him on the forehead. Some children are excited by His appearance and cry out, "Boo! boo!"

The traveler does not become disturbed, but a sad expression is on His face, and tears come to His eyes. Having reached the churchyard, He turns toward the main entrance of the church. Immovable and with hands stretched out, He pronounces the awesome words, *hoc est enim corpus meum*: "This is My Body." The priest at that moment consecrates the Host. In the church, angel voices are praising the thrice holy God. The Man dressed in fustian goes toward the hill country. There, on the summit of the hill, in a solitary place, rises an old wayside cross. The importunate beggar who was refused everywhere places His wallet on the ground; it opens and a great number of disdained Hosts escape from it which shine on the sand like stars. Then He removes His robe, and

Uncommon Virtue

His Body, girded with a loin cloth, looks striped from the wounds of the flagellation. Soon, invisible hammers resound; nails thrust themselves into the feet of the Man and fix Him to the Cross. A woman, unnoticed till then, remains near the Cross. In this mystery of sorrow and of love, her heart is transfixed, and her blood mingles with the Blood which flows from the Crucified. The distance is lost to infinity, filled with multitudes looking east toward the agonizing victim. The greater part show only indifference; some affect disdain; others triumphant pride; many shake their fists; while, very close to the bloody Cross, John and the Cyrenean and a little group of women in which are discerned Mary Magdalen and Veronica seem to desire by the intensity of their love to compensate for all the forgetfulness and ingratitude, for all the injuries, the ignominy, and all the innumerable atrocities.

A simple scene thought up and more or less fictionalized? Alas, no! It is rather a powerful evocation of the reality of every day: A God who offers Himself, ungrateful hearts who refuse Him, brutal persons who injure Him, former faithful ones who blaspheme or desert; only a small group who understands the opportunity, the urgent necessity, of compensating for all that flood or infamy, of *making reparation*.

Love of Reparation

If one desires an authentic story, is it not enough to recall the earnest requests of our Savior made to Margaret Mary?[58] Certainly, the apparitions to the Visitandine nun of Paray-le-Monial[59] have neither historically nor dogmatically established the doctrine of reparation, as we have

[58] 1647, birth, July 22, at Vesrovres, in Charolais. Her father was Claude Alacoque, notary.
1671, entered the convent of the Visitation at Parey (May 25).
1674, beginning of the principal communications with God; the arrival of Fr. Claude de la Colombière as superior at the residence of the Jesuits at Paray.
1675, the great revelation of the Sacred Heart, during the octave of Corpus Christi.
1690, died October 17, at the age of forty-three.
1715, first information concerning the virtues and miracles of the servant of God, then a century passes (Jansenism, philosophism, revolution).
1817, the cause is introduced.
1846, declared venerable.
1864, beatification.
1925, canonization. The body of the saint is, as we know, preserved at Paray in the chapel of the Visitation. It is enclosed in a reliquary, of which more than half of the cost was paid by Belgian Catholics.

[59] This commune receives its name le Monial, "the nun," because it was once home to an old Benedictine convent. The convent church, which was constructed in about the year 1004, serves at the present time as the parish church.

already remarked; but they emphasize the opportunity for reparation. There were as many as seventy manifestations of the Sacred Heart to the humble religious. The apparition which summarizes the others is this one, which the saint herself relates thus:

"One day, when the Blessed Sacrament was exposed, our Lord manifested Himself to me brilliant with glory, His five wounds shining like five suns.... From this sacred humanity came forth flames from all parts, but especially from His adorable breast, which resembled a furnace." And behold, His breast opened and revealed "His loving and amiable Heart, the living source of these flames." The Savior displayed to the humble, prostrate daughter "the inexplicable wonders" of His pure love and even to what excess He had carried it out of love for men. But, alas! He received in return "only ingratitude and lack of appreciation." That was much more painful to Him than all He had suffered in His Passion. "If men rendered Me," He continued, "some return of love, I should esteem little all I have done for them, and should wish, if such could be, to suffer it over again; but they meet My eager love only with coldness and rebuffs."

Thus, an immense love has presided at our salvation. Since this immense love is disregarded, it is necessary to

Love of Reparation

make amends. Or, if you like, infinite Love must ask for love. This love the creature refuses Him. It is for Christians of good will to love "for them," in their personal name first and then for all those who refuse love.

In a play by Emile Augier,[60] we see two brothers, Bernard and Leopold. Leopold does not know the blood bond that exists between him and Bernard. The latter renders to Leopold, who is so closely related to him, many services. As a result of misunderstanding, Leopold chances to strike his benefactor in the face. Bernard reveals to his brother the tie that unites them. Leopold is heartbroken, but Bernard opens his arms and holds out his cheek, saying, "Wipe it away!"

How easy the application! Till now, perhaps, we have not understood the fraternal tie which unites us to Jesus Christ. The encyclical has come at an opportune time to refresh our memory. Or else, it was a reading, a communion, a reflection, or the thought of the evil which is increasing around us that has done this.

We have no longer the right to be ignorant. Our Lord shows us every thorn of His crown, the inexhaustible alms purse of His pierced hands. He asks us, He pleads with

---

[60] "The House of Fourchambault."

us to make compensation, reparation: "You, at least, can wipe this away!"

Look at the innumerable sins which are committed around you. You are willing, are you not? Wipe them away! Look at the terrible sins of omission of all those who forget God. Wipe them also away!

Look at the devastating work of the enemies of the Church. It is always the battle between two cities, but often, the children of darkness seem to have more zeal or intelligence than the children of light. Are you willing to repulse the powers of evil by your prayers and renunciations? Wipe all that away!

And there are also the many hardworking laborers who are so far from Me! That is My keenest disappointment. I have a special preference for those whom life treats more rigorously, but the majority of the working class no longer know Me, no longer love Me. Do you wipe that away?

Who would resist listening to this touching appeal?

The practice of reparation

Let us show in a few words this doctrine, how to live it; this duty, how to practice it.

According to the nature of things, reparation will be, in accordance with an authorized division, either *affective*, *effective*, or *afflictive*. According to the inclination of his soul to the call of grace, each one will be drawn toward the form of reparation that he prefers. The perfect form will draw inspiration from all three ways, with a shifting of emphasis on this or that way, according to the circumstances.

Let us consider each separately for the sake of clarification:

Affective reparation. This is made especially by prayer and by love. On beholding the supernatural situation of the world, the soul is thrown into a state of anguish. Then, at the feet of God, she deplores this distressing state; she offers herself to make reparation for the abyss of sin; she cries out as did the seraph of Assisi: "Jesus is not loved, Jesus is not loved!" Great desires rise in her to love in the place of all those who do not love, to pray for all those who do not pray, to adore for those who do not adore, to offer an act of ardent love for each blasphemy that is uttered, a diamond of the purest water for each rent in the mantle of the Church. In the world around me, the Kingdom of God does not come; but in me, at least, it will come to the maximum! God is driven from so many hearts; in mine, He will have the largest place. Jesus our Savior is not known enough; I, at least, shall apply myself in the secret of an assiduous contemplation to know Him intimately.

Uncommon Virtue

Effective Reparation. I do not content myself with singing. I enter the lists, and then, "To work!" How can I serve? Where do they need my assistance? In the fulfillment of the duty of my state, where Providence has placed me, is it there that the divine Head, of whom I am a vital and living member, looks to me for the establishment of His Kingdom? But what am I going to do to save the world?

Perhaps there is nothing to modify in the *plan* of my life. But can I not animate my whole life with another *spirit*, cause love to penetrate all my actions, and quietly insert there as an obsession the haunting memory of the souls who are lost and who by me, by this insignificant detail of my life today, can be saved or sanctified? It is perhaps not the question of doing *something else*, but of doing *otherwise*. This is effective reparation.

There remains *afflictive reparation*. No longer only a matter of compensating prayer; no longer only, in the plan of the duty of one's state, the direct apostolate to unite, reunite, or unite more closely to Christ the souls that surround us. Sin consists in an undue pleasure that the creature accords to himself. In view to repair this undue pleasure, I shall impose upon myself a proportionate suffering, and this, united vitally to the redemptive sacrifice, will have redemptive value.

Love of Reparation

Man seeks only sensuality; I shall compensate for it by mortifying my senses. The world thrives on excess; in the balance, I shall place my own privations. The world holds mortification in horror; I shall make war on the search for comforts. That these formulas may not remain mere formulas but may become in a Christian life a living thing, continually practiced and lived, we need something more than a little burst of enthusiasm.

A last word. "Very willingly," someone will say, "I shall attempt to make reparation for others. But alas! when I look at myself, my past appears to me so overwhelming that there will not be too much of all my compensating efforts to atone for my personal offenses. How am I going to burden myself with those of others? I have so much reparation to make—and this every day—for my own sins."

If one would speak in that way, would he not show a certain pusillanimity, a sort of spiritual egoism, in which perhaps the glory of God has less place than appears?

Doubtless there are many shortcomings in every life. It is necessary to exert oneself energetically to overcome them and to make up for them. But a fig for a spirituality which does not go beyond oneself! Forget yourself for a moment. Think of other souls. You are a part of Christ. Think of all that is, or should be, a part of Christ. Besides, do you not believe that the best way to arouse oneself to the maximum of personal perfection is to work to the maximum for the perfection of others?

When one is conscious of his responsibility for saving souls, he has on his lips the words of St. Christopher: "It is heavy to bear." But if he is courageous, he will at the same time have in his heart the desire to unleash his forces. The more a man realizes that he is an apostle, the more he aspires to become a saint. To think of others is the noble way of working for oneself.

Moreover, God would be very powerless or very inconsiderate if He allowed you to be condemned for your generosity toward your neighbor. Do not be afraid. Jesus does not let Himself be outdone. Is He not able to help one who is most willing to help Him save the world?

VIII

Pity for the Sick and Afflicted

An Invalid, Apostle of Invalids

Jacqueline Bellioque died peacefully in 1944 at the age of fifty. Her illness had begun thirty-five years before.

In view of the fact that she was an artist, a musician, a lover of all that is beautiful and elevating, refined, genteel, and gifted with an indisputable charm, life seemed to have smiled on her. But it was at that moment that a malady of multiple forms and of most disabling effects seized her.

She was treated as a nervous case by doctors who were completely baffled by the strange character of her illness. Consequently, she was all the more misunderstood by the members of her own family, since her mother had died a long time before and was thus missing from the home. She made extraordinary efforts to bear up in the midst of these terrible sufferings. Only a younger sister understood her, but she could not make her opinion prevail. Later, when the sister was married, far away from home, and had six children, she could not be of any assistance to Jacqueline. How great moral sufferings does such a league of incomprehension represent!

All this entered into God's designs, as did all her work for the sick that was its result. This was a truly fruitful work. By means of her correspondence, she reached many persons from her bed. Timid and unobtrusive in ordinary life, Jacqueline dared everything when it was a question of her dear sick. In the course of a pilgrimage to Lourdes, she succeeded in entertaining personally Cardinal Jorio with her work. She did not hesitate to write to ecclesiastical personages in the highest positions, provided she found there some advantage for her work.

From numerous confidences received from her beloved sick, Jacqueline noticed that besides the physical and moral suffering, there existed another suffering of a spiritual order: the sick were being deprived of the Holy Eucharist. This concerned her deeply. She left no stone unturned in order to make known in high circles actual facts and the number of sick concerned. As evidence, we have her remarkable notes relative to the Communion of the sick and the little work

Pity for the Sick and Afflicted

"Frequent Communion of the Sick," which was recently published. Her charitable and bold attempts have already had appreciable results, of which many sick are the happy beneficiaries at the present time. Among her successes are daily Communion in various hospitals and Communion brought to the sick by deacons in certain large centers.

Many will wish to read over again or learn to know the beautiful prayer composed by the valiant apostle:

> My Lord Jesus Christ, who during Thy mortal life didst not cease to bend over the sick to console them and to cure them, I beseech Thee, with all the fervor of my soul, to continue Thy compassionate visits by granting them to be able to receive Thee as often as possible in the sacrament of Thy love.

In the month of June 1943, Jacqueline's state of health became a source for alarm. She received Extreme Unction and sent for the sister who understood her. The crisis passed, but the blow given to her health was very severe. From that moment, her sufferings increased in proportion as a certain strange but true phenomenon increased. It was proved later that when she slept for a certain time, all the functions of her body became sluggish. She then had to fight against peaceful sleep.

Uncommon Virtue

The attacks became more and more strong and frequent. She passed in a few hours from an apparent state of improvement to a most alarming condition.

In December 1943, it was thought that the end was near. Jacqueline had double pneumonia, but in a strange way, this pulmonary congestion was cured. However, certain swellings which had previously appeared became more pronounced, and the poor patient, being scarcely able to move in her bed, had to renounce forever putting her foot on the ground. As long as she possibly could, she had continued to get up in order to render herself indispensable services, knowing well that otherwise she would not have the necessary help.

"When I reached her, on February 21, 1944," writes her sister, "there had just arisen in her body such a bloated condition that those who approached her literally got the impression that she was going to burst. Seeing this, Jacqueline, whose doctor usually was absent, asked for a surgeon who was passing through Besse. He believed that he had discovered an enormous cancer, and he told us of his diagnosis. We all came, my husband and my children, in order to see again for a last time our loved invalid. Shortly after our arrival, the excessive swelling had made the skin of the abdomen break open, and there oozed

Pity for the Sick and Afflicted

out several liters of liquid. This relieved Jacqueline but weakened her very much."

The disease affected her body everywhere: her right leg was almost paralyzed; her disordered abdomen caused continual discomposure, and in her condition, this must have been very painful. Her tongue was parched and was cracking in every part, and during the last days, her eyes began to suppurate. As to the cancer, it was found out that she did not have it. It was also believed that she had uremia, but an analysis of her blood did not reveal any urea. Her malady was therefore not definitely determined until the end.

One of her greatest sacrifices, if not the greatest, was to see all her notes and documents removed from her bedside for the convenience of giving her care. She understood the need for this, but yet it was hard for her! She felt that was a definite farewell to her cherished work, which she had performed for such a long time in spite of her suffering and which she ceased only fifteen days before her death.

Her solicitude for the sick continued up to the last moment. Observing that her companions in suffering did not receive the attention which would have helped them, she pointed out to her sister how the little remedies she tried on herself in order to alleviate her pain could also be used to their advantage for comfort and relief.

Uncommon Virtue

If the physical sufferings of Jacqueline were intense, her spiritual sufferings were no less so. She found herself in a state of such spiritual darkness and dreadful uneasiness that she trembled at the thought of the judgment of God, preserving confidence only in the innermost depths of her heart.

When a crisis which was considered the last came, she called for a priest and asked him for a final absolution. The prayers for the dying were said while she was completely conscious. After that, she experienced a great spiritual consolation, for she had always feared that she would die without having had all the spiritual aids of our holy religion.

Then, she very briefly but very humbly asked pardon of all. However, God did not yet want her. On the following day, imminent danger had passed, and she was very much surprised to have still to go on living. It distressed her and frightened her a little: "What does the good God still demand of me? I was already at death's door."

The interior martyrdom still continued. It seemed to her that she was an outcast, a detestable person in the sight of God, and that if God granted her the least place in Heaven, that would still be too good for her. Her soul no longer felt anything, no longer saw anything, and this

Pity for the Sick and Afflicted

distressed her greatly. "She asked me to pray with her," writes her sister, "and for this great soul, I looked for the most elevating, the most universal prayers; to open her wings fully, I spoke to her for a long time about the Mystical Body of Christ. This consoled and comforted her. One would have said that she could no longer think of anything by herself, and accordingly, as I would suggest thoughts to her, she would say with relief: 'Oh! It is true, it is true.'"

About the fifth day before her death, she declared: "This is not yet the light, but it is less dark." One time, when they made her take a cooling drink, she stopped to say: "I have just had an inspiration regarding charity toward one's neighbor and the spirit of union. It is the first chapter of the 'Rivers of Living Waters' which has suggested it to me. The lack of charity is more serious than all the rest. Dissension makes God depart; it is so serious that I ask myself whether even mortifications can atone for that. Anyhow, let us hope so." But she seemed not to be too sure about it.

On another occasion, she said: "There is a little light manifesting itself, but it is difficult to explain." She was advised not to try but to continue to profit peacefully by the grace which was sent to her, and it has not been known what she had perceived.

Uncommon Virtue

To reassure her, they spoke to her about the merits she had acquired by her years of suffering. When they said to her, "You have suffered so much," she used to answer with an unforgettable, impressive, and confusing "Oh, yes!" Were they not facing with her an ocean, an abyss of immolation? The second day before she died, the expression on her face was absolutely heart-rending. It seemed that she personified all the sufferings of her beloved sick for whom she had offered for a long time the trials of her disease and now her life.

After another warning, the ups and downs in her state of health continued, but at about 4:00 p.m. on the second day before she died, she had such an attack of weakness that the prayers for the dying and the last invocations were again recited. She no longer reacted to anything, not even to ether, and thus she remained unconscious for a long time. Finally she revived, but she who up to that time had been aware of the least details was delirious until the next morning.

At the time of a favorable change in her condition, her sister offered to give her a short spiritual reading, which she generally liked very much. Not finding what she desired in what was suggested to her, she said, "Speak to me rather about your children; that will fatigue me less."

Pity for the Sick and Afflicted

A pious soul came to see her. Jacqueline began to speak of her death. It still seemed to her that she had done nothing for God and that she would go before Him empty-handed. She feared that her activity may have been carried on only for the sake of appearances and not out of pure love of God. She was told that the best proof of her pure intention was that she had suffered so terribly for the difficult and delicate mission which God had entrusted to her that she certainly would not have consented to suffer so much if she had not deeply loved Him. That reassured her. It may be said that there came to her mind nothing of what could have been in her favor. With deep gratitude, she accepted any word of encouragement.

On the eve of her death, although she seemed to be better, when I spoke to her about her Holy Communion the following day, she said to me: "Tomorrow morning is far off ... if you knew.... Another world will dawn for me before tomorrow morning."

Indeed, she did not have the happiness of receiving the hoped-for Holy Communion of the next day; she died during the *night*. The nurse on duty assisted her in her last moments.

Uncommon Virtue

In the service of those who suffer

We see the magnanimity of those who have to endure suffering, but this must not make us forget the magnanimity of the chosen souls who consecrate themselves to the service of the sick.

In *The Magic Mountain*, Thomas Mann alludes in passing to the personnel in charge of the sick. He sketches with one stroke of his pen this rather unsympathetic picture: "A nurse appears somewhere in her white cap, wearing on her nose a pince-nez of which the cord passed behind her ear. She was apparently a Protestant nun, without a true vocation for her work, fastidious, agitated, and distressed by ennui."

Far from us be the thought that this depiction provides an accurate character portrait. We know several Protestant nursing-homes, and we must say that they are maintained with a devotion equal to that of our own religious.

But without wanting to judge by way of comparison, no one, I think, will refuse to our Catholic religious devoted to the care of the sick a certificate of unmixed devotion, of first-rate competence, and of ardent love for their vocation. We wish to express on our part what our admiration has been each time it was our privilege to see at close range

Pity for the Sick and Afflicted

hospitals, sanatoriums, or clinics. Sisters of Charity, Sisters of Niederbronn, Sisters of St. Joseph, Religious of Lyon, Blue Sisters of Castres, Franciscans of Calais, Sisters of St. Martha of Angoulême, Religious of Nevers, and many others could be mentioned, but we do not know to whom the palm should be awarded.

Whatever their class may be, and whatever repugnance they may offer to poor human nature, the suffering members of Christ find generous souls who consecrate their lives to the service of their infirmity.

Let us see the most magnanimous among these souls at work. May they pardon our boldness if our poor lines offer them some slight recognition.

Seekers of love

George Sand[61] relates in her *Histoire de ma vie* how when she was a little girl, there came now and then to Nohant a poor boy who had gone mad as a result of a disappointment in love. He did not ask anybody anything but wandered about aimlessly in the garden and sometimes ventured to

[61] Amantine Lucile Aurore Dupin (1804–1876), the Baroness Dudevant, pen name George Sand, was a French writer.

go into the house. When he was asked what he wanted, he answered: "Nothing new, *I am looking for love.*" "You have not yet found it?" "No, but I have searched everywhere. I do not know where it can be." "Have you searched in the garden?" "No, not yet." Struck by a sudden idea, he made his way to the garden, where in his madness, he went from tree to tree along the paths, looking for love.

This memory of the Baroness Dudevant came back to me one day as I was conducting in an old folks home a retreat for two communities of the Little Sisters of the Poor, who were gathered there because of the war.

I had no business with the good old men or the good old women there. However, on leaving the chaplain's residence in order to reach the room where the exercises were held, or while I took a little fresh air along the walks, I met poor wrinkled faces, figures bent in two, going toward a sunny corner with tottering steps. I admired the impression of repose and peaceful happiness in all these men and women, worn out by age and infirmities. Certainly, I conjectured that here or there rheumatism was deep-rooted, that elsewhere were verified traces of palsy in spite of the valiant efforts to dissimulate the trembling of legs and hands; but there were no long faces, rather joyful, beaming countenances, in spite of the wrinkles and trials poorly dissimulated.

Pity for the Sick and Afflicted

I said to myself: "What have these old people come to look for here? Probably repose for the body, care in case of illness. But especially, a little affection and love for hearts that life has undoubtedly treated rudely."

It is not that many of them could not have had or did not actually have their share of love in life. Once, at home, their mothers lavished attention and caresses upon them; later in their homes, which almost every one of them founded, they shared the joys of married life.

But all that is so long ago! Even when the skin of the face has shriveled up, the heart does not cease to need love. Where is one to find this love, when one has no longer any charms to offer or when, because of certain infirmities, one is no longer anything but a heavy burden to the family or relatives? Surely, this one or that one would have found in the family atmosphere, with a son or daughter, a home in his old age. But how do materially sufficient attentions—since by hypothesis it is a question of poor surroundings—compare with spiritually uplifting attentions?

God thought of that and a century ago inspired Jeanne Jugan[62] to make the admirable foundation of the Little Sisters of the Poor. Homes for the aged were established

---

[62] Jeanne Jugan was canonized in 2009.

where they devote body and soul to the poor old people and where they seek through the tenderest and strongest supernatural motives to create for them a home of holy affection.

"What do you seek when you pass over this threshold, my good old man, my good old lady?... Do not answer me. I understand. You are coming to seek a little love. Pass the threshold without any fear. From the good Mother to the least of the little Sisters, everyone will overwhelm you with warm affection. Come in! Come in! Welcome!"

While I was conducting the retreat, an excellent old woman died at the women's infirmary. She was ninety-four years old, a vigorous Alsatian whom life seemed to leave regretfully. I asked the assistant Sister who was serving my meals for information regarding her. "I wanted to get up," she answered, "between midnight and one o'clock, because that is the difficult time when death approaches. I awakened at 11:30; my good little woman was calm and needed only to be raised again on her pillows; undoubtedly, the great day for her will be tomorrow! Another little old woman in the infirmary is failing also; she was thirsty but did not want to take a drink because the chaplain had promised to bring her Holy Communion in the morning and she thought it was after midnight. After I informed her about the correct time, she drank very willingly. See how edifying our dear old people are," the assistant Sister added with a smile, so as to make me forget what I admired particularly, her devotion to her patient in this nocturnal adventure.

Assuredly, there may arise sometimes, in one or the other refectory, some disputes, some little jealousies. But the Little Sister on duty quickly pacifies the souls and applies balm where she finds a little hard friction. A single order predominates entirely in the home: charity.

Jeanne Jugan and her daughters have understood Christ. The parable of the vine and the branches is not a dead letter for these souls. Christ is the whole Christ; and the members of Christ merit a cult similar to that which one owes to Christ the Head: "as long as you did it to one of these my least brethren, you did it to me" (Matt. 25:40). The thought of this ineffable reality is what gives courage to the Little Sisters of the Poor. We were speaking of their love for the old people; the word "love" must be considered with all the maternal meaning that it comprises. It is not a matter of a love which a little of merely human pity could explain. It is a matter of a supernatural love. Every old man or woman is a member of Christ. Why not consecrate the best of one's heart to these suffering members whom life has treated so harshly?

Uncommon Virtue

Ah! Young women who are dreaming of a life of pure faith, of ardent charity, of devotion with the least possible human recompense but the maximum supernatural joy, do not forget that there are novitiates of the Little Sisters of the Poor and that they are calling for reinforcements!

The most forsaken

When from the plateau on which the town of Rodez is proudly situated, we look toward the south, in the direction of Segala, we notice at some kilometers to the right a series of imposing buildings with red roofs. It is the Cayssiols asylum.

About forty Religious devote themselves there to the service of six hundred persons whom various mental afflictions have constrained to be separated from ordinary life. Out of delicacy to the patients, we are not, as a rule, admitted to visit there. But thanks to my cassock and the courtesy of the kind Superior, the doors were opened to me, and I wish to tell what a deep impression I received from that visit.

The plan is unique: close to the edge of the plateau which overlooks the deep valley of Aveyron, one enjoys a splendid view of Rodez. The summit of the ornate tower of its rose-colored cathedral is crowned with a statue of the Virgin, protectress of the whole region.

Pity for the Sick and Afflicted

The practical installations in the various buildings and its services are the last word of its kind. Without doubt, Cayssiols is the most beautiful asylum in France, and perhaps in the world. It has electrical equipment in kitchen and laundry, a place for hydrotherapeutics, a pharmacy, and an operating room. There are fine dormitories which two Sisters every night, at the least noise, survey from their room through a dormer window which is almost imperceptible and resembles a simple opening for ventilation. There are large shops for work and airy covered walks and gardens adjacent to each building. Everything is done to give the patients the greatest comfort in absolute security.

Every morning, the doctor makes his visit to all the buildings. If there are any new emergency cases, he prescribes the proper treatment. I asked the Sister Superior, "Do you get any appreciable improvements?" "Certainly," she replied, "besides hydrotherapy, which has been known for a long time and is a great help, we have found that new products, among which may be mentioned insulin, and certain chemical remedies effect marvelous results. Just today, two persons, after only one month of treatment, have left the house, completely cured." "What is the proportion of the patients who can be cured and of those who remain sunk in insanity?" "We can count on cures being effected in almost 40 percent." "And the causes, Mother?" "Oh! Ever so many! Heredity, which is the most obstinate to cure, traumatism; occasionally, any cause whatsoever: sorrow, intemperance, bad conduct…" "And among your patients, are there some who have sufficient soundness of mind to fulfill their religious duties?" "We have about fifteen Communions every morning, about forty on certain feasts. There have been fifty Easter Communions this year. You see, that is a good number! The chaplain of the Institute is not without certain consolations!"

I inquired of the religious about their rule and motives of their vocation.

They are the Sisters of St. Mary of the Assumption, whose motherhouse is in Clermont-Ferrand. They have numerous foundations: Privas, Le Puy, Nice. Their founder was Fr. Chiron, who was named in 1825 by the bishop of Viviers, Msgr. Bonnet, to be chaplain of the prison of Privas. At that time, those who were mentally ill lived in the same quarters as those condemned by the courts of justice. Fr. Chiron found this situation abnormal. Seven young women from a village of Ardèche, where he had previously exercised his ministry, were the first recruits of the new Institute, which at present takes care of six thousand patients. The government did not hesitate a

Pity for the Sick and Afflicted

few years ago to award the cross of the Legion of Honor to the Mother General in order to thank all the Sisters in her person for their inexpressible devotion.

While I was returning to Rodez by way of the picturesque town of Olemps, where stands the castle of the Rodat family, a name that also evokes a beautiful religious foundation, I asked myself, as my eyes beheld the color of the sunlight on the cathedral emerging from the city like a great ship, why God should not cause holy vocations to spring up here or there in order to come to reinforce the novitiate of the Sisters of St. Mary of the Assumption.

A cathedral surmounted by a Madonna; a life dominated by the Virgin. The parallel was striking. But as a solid stone is necessary for the cathedral in order not to break off under the burning sun and not to wear down under the rain and wind of winter days, so a solid stone is also necessary for the holy vocations which decide to consecrate themselves for life to the care of the mentally afflicted. With children, there is youth. With ordinary patients and the aged, some possibility for receiving gratitude, however rare this may be. Here, nothing for nature, neither a kind smile on the part of the poor patient nor gratitude. Occasionally, there is instead, in the excess of some agitation, a blow, a threat. In other words, all, absolutely all, is for God alone.

Uncommon Virtue

How wonderful it is that there are souls generous enough to devote themselves to such work! May they find here the homage merited by the example that they give and that the world knows so little. We pray that the Sisters of St. Mary of the Assumption may be better known by the public; that among young women, more than one may be won by the thought of going to the aid of the mentally ill; and that priests charged with the guidance of vocations may direct some of them to this sublime way of consecrating oneself to one's neighbor.

About the Author

Fr. Raoul Plus, S.J. (1882-1958), wrote more than forty books to help Christians understand God's love for the soul. His works stress the vital role of prayer in the spiritual life and show how you can live the truths of the Faith. A native of France, Fr. Plus studied abroad because of the 1901 laws against religious orders. As a French army chaplain during World War I, he gave the soldiers talks that were to serve as the material for his first two books, *Dieu en nous* (*God within Us*) and *L'Idée reparatrice* (*Ideal of Reparation*), which were translated into numerous languages. For his wartime services, Plus was decorated with the *croix de guerre*. Fr. Plus served as professor of religion and spiritual director at the Université Catholique at Lille and taught at the Institut Catholique in Paris. He was also a renowned preacher and retreat master.

Sophia Institute

Sophia Institute is a nonprofit institution that seeks to nurture the spiritual, moral, and cultural life of souls and to spread the gospel of Christ in conformity with the authentic teachings of the Roman Catholic Church.

Sophia Institute Press fulfills this mission by offering translations, reprints, and new publications that afford readers a rich source of the enduring wisdom of mankind.

Sophia Institute also operates the popular online resource CatholicExchange.com. *Catholic Exchange* provides world news from a Catholic perspective as well as daily devotionals and articles that will help readers to grow in holiness and live a life consistent with the teachings of the Church.

In 2013, Sophia Institute launched Sophia Institute for Teachers to renew and rebuild Catholic culture through service to Catholic education. With the goal of nurturing the spiritual, moral, and cultural life of souls, and an abiding respect for the role and work of teachers, we strive to provide materials and programs that are at once enlightening to the mind and ennobling to the heart; faithful and complete, as well as useful and practical.

Sophia Institute gratefully recognizes the Solidarity Association for preserving and encouraging the growth of our apostolate over the course of many years. Without their generous and timely support, this book would not be in your hands.

www.SophiaInstitute.com
www.CatholicExchange.com
www.SophiaInstituteforTeachers.org

Sophia Institute Press® is a registered trademark of Sophia Institute.
Sophia Institute is a tax-exempt institution as defined by the
Internal Revenue Code, Section 501(c)(3). Tax ID 22-2548708.